NINJA FOODI COOKBOOK

Tasty & Flavorful Recipes for Indoor Crisping with your Ninja Foodi

BY

Michael Francis

ISBN: 978-1-952504-68-6

COPYRIGHT © 2020 by Michael Francis

All rights reserved. This book is copyright protected and it's for personal use only. Without the prior written permission of the publisher, no part of this publication should be reproduced, distributed, or transmitted in any form or by any means, including photocopying, recording, or other electronic or mechanical methods.

This publication is sold with the idea that the publisher is not required to render accounting, officially permitted, or otherwise, qualified services. If advice is required, it is necessary to seek the services of a legal or professional, a practiced individual in the profession. This document is geared towards providing substantial and reliable information in regards to the topics covered.

DISCLAIMER

The information written in this book is for educational and entertainment purposes only. Strenuous efforts have been made to provide accurate, up to date and reliable complete information. The information in this book is true and complete to the best of our knowledge. All recommendations are made without guarantee on the part of the author and publisher.

Neither the publisher nor the author takes any responsibility for any possible consequences of reading or enjoying the recipes in this book. The author and publisher disclaim any liability in connection with the use of information contained in this book. Under no circumstance will any legal responsibility or blame be apportioned against the author or publisher for any reparation, damages, or monetary loss due to the information herein, either directly or indirectly.

Table of Contents

INTRODUCTION 8

Meaning of Ninja Foodi 9

Benefit of Using Ninja Foodi 10

Function Buttons of Your Ninja Foodi 12

Ninja Foodi Pressure Releasing Method 14

Steps to Use Your Ninja Foodi 15

Useful Tips for Using Your Ninja Foodi 16

Ninja Foodi Trouble Shooting 17

Ninja Foodi Frequently Asked Questions and Answers 19

NINJA FOODI BREAKFAST RECIPES 21

    Pretzel Bites 21

    Hash Brown Casserole 23

    French Toast Casserole 24

    Apple Pie Monkey Bread Muffins 25

    Cookies 26

    Pot Roast 28

    Oatmeal 30

    Homemade Bread 31

    Frozen Egg Rolls 33

    Green Tomatoes 34

    Sausage 35

    Pumpkin Zucchini Muffins 36

    Sweet Potato Breakfast Hash 37

    Scrambled Eggs 38

NINJA FOODI POULTRY RECIPES 40

Asian Shredded Chicken 40

Buffalo Chicken Wings 41

Root Beer Chicken Wings 42

Chicken Satay 43

Buffalo and Ranch Wings 45

Chicken Enchiladas 46

Mexican Shredded Chicken 47

Jalapeno Hot Popper and Chicken Dip 49

Crack Chicken 50

Cracked up Tator Tots with Chicken 51

30 Minutes Fall Off the Bone Ribs 52

NINJA FOODI BEEF & PORK RECIPES 53

Tender BBQ Ribs 53

Parmesan Pork Chops 54

Bacon Ranch Beef Stroganoff 56

Pork Tenderloin Green Beans 57

Italian Beef and Rice 58

Lasagna Shells with Meat Sauce 59

Pork Chops 60

Perfect Roast Beef 62

Prime Rib 63

Pulled Pork 64

NINJA FOODI FISH & SEAFOOD RECIPES 66

Coconut Shrimp 66

Balsamic Shrimp and Sausage 68

Cajun Shrimp 70

- Chili Lime Shrimp 72
- Salmon Patties 74
- Shrimp Boil 76

NINJA FOODI SOUP RECIPES 78

- Corn Chowder 78
- French Onion Soup Chicken Bake 80
- Taco Soup 81
- Alphabet Vegetable Soup 83
- Anasazi Bean and Ham Hock Soup 84
- Autumn Soup 85
- Easy Clam Chowder 86
- Bacon Cheeseburger Soup 87
- Bear Creek Cheddar Potato Soup Mix 89
- Beef and Barley Soup 90

NINJA FOODI RICE & PASTA RECIPES 91

- Spaghetti Bolognese Sauce 91
- Spanish Rice 93
- Quick Chicken and Rice 94
- Mac and Cheese with Bacon 96
- Taco Pasta Bake 98
- Cajun Sausage Pasta Bake 100
- Mexican Rice 102
- Pepperoni Pasta Salad 104
- Queso Mac and Cheese with Spicy Ground Beef 106
- Healthy Pasta Salad 108

NINJA FOODI BEANS & GRAIN RECIPES 110

Corn on the Cob 110

Green Beans 111

Barbequed Baked Beans 112

Black Bean and Beef Taco Soup 114

Black Bean Chili 116

Black-Eyed Peas Chili 117

Baked Beans 118

Anasazi Bean and Ham Hock Soup 120

NINJA FOODI VEGETABLE RECIPES 121

Brussels Sprouts 121

Toasted Israeli Couscous with Vegetables 122

Charred Vegetable and Couscous Salad 124

Buffalo Cauliflower 126

Saffron, Courgette and Herb Couscous 127

Seasoned Asparagus 129

Steak and Vegetable Bowls 130

Vidalia Onions 131

Roasted Carrots 132

NINJA FOODI APPETIZER RECIPES 133

Homemade Peanut Sauce 133

Crab Rangoon 134

Meatballs 135

Oreos 137

Football Deviled Eggs 138

Lasagna Dip 139

Peanut Butter Cups 140

Roasted Garlic 141

Peppers 142

Pineapple Sweet and Sour Sauce 143

NINJA FOODI DESSERT RECIPES 144

Apple Fritter 144

Domino's Cinnamon Bread Twists 146

Pumpkin Pie Custard Cups 148

Brownies 149

Christmas Tree Brownies 151

Baked Drunken Apples 153

5 Ingredients Pumpkin Cake 155

Apple Cobbler 156

Banana Cupcakes 157

Chocolate Lava Cake 158

INTRODUCTION

Nowadays people fall in love with crispy foods. Most pressure cookers cannot cook crispy foods but Ninja Foodi has attempted to close this gap. It does this through its air crisping function. This function supports Air Frying and Dehydrating mode as well. The Ninja Foodi would be a good choice if you always like to Air-fry and dehydrate in order to get a crispy skin on your chicken.

Most pressure cookers works according to their programmed control panels. Ninja Foodi's control panel is one of the clearest and concise panels ever tested. Simple arrow buttons adjust temperature and time, and there are buttons assigned for selecting each one of its functions. Some models complicate the control panel by creating diverse settings for beef, soup, chicken etc.

The Ninja Foodi is built with the capacity to cook food faster than the traditional cooking method and then makes use of the crisp function to give your food a perfect finish. In the other hand, the Ninja Foodi crisping function needs two separate lids. One for pressure cooker while the other one for crisping purpose.

Meaning of Ninja Foodi

Ninja Foodi is a kitchen appliance used in cooking many kinds of food. It is a pressure cooker and an Air Fryer which cooks food and give you a crispy and perfect result. The Ninja Foodi however can also be used as an oven, slow cooker, dehydrator, steamer or roaster.

The crisping function of the Ninja Foodi makes it unique and different from other pressure cookers. In order to achieve the crispness, Ninja Foodi has two different lids. These are: a detachable pressure cooking lid for tenderness and a non-removable crisping lid.

Similarly, the Ninja Foodi works like an Instant Pot and other electric pressure cookers and the unit is very easy to operate. For instance the display window which shows you what's going on inside the pot looks very nice. It shows you how much time is left to complete the cooking and also gives you hints to lock the lid.

Benefit of Using Ninja Foodi

1. **Ninja Foodi gives a Healthier Cooking.**

It is true that Frying food with oil is not healthy but Ninja Foodi can fry food with little or no oil. Using oil is a personal choice, not mandatory. Food cooked with the Ninja Foodi is healthy and crispy even without adding oil. Food for cooked with the Ninja Foodi is crispier than the ones cooked with the traditional oven.

2. **Ninja Foodi Delivers Quick and Perfect Meals.**

Ninja Foodi is known for its unique feature of cooking food faster and delicious. It does this by circulating hot air around the food. The traditional oven may take up to 30 minutes to come to pressure whereas Ninja Foodi takes some few minutes to come to pressure. The traditional oven may take up to 45 minutes to properly cook frozen fries but Ninja Foodi can cook frozen fries within 10 to 15 minutes.

3. **Ninja Foodi is Versatile.**

The Ninja Foodi has the capacity to do many things. It can cook frozen fries, and cake. It can also grill, broil, stir fry and roast. The Ninja Foodi is very easy to operate and you can also use it to Cook fresh and frozen food including leftover, meat, fish, casseroles, sandwiches and a lot of different veggies. There is some Ninja Foodi models that come with grill pan or elevated cooking basket. Dividable baskets mean you have the opportunity to cook many things at the same time. It is impressive that one unit can cook so many things in so diverse ways.

4. **It is Not Difficult to Use.**

Operating the Ninja Foodi is very simple. You do not need to perform lots of settings. You just need to set the cooking time, temperature, put the food and then you start cooking. You do not necessarily need to stir the food while cooking unlike cooking with stove top which requires you to stir. The basket helps shaking your food to be simple and fast. The unit however doesn't lose a lot of heat when you open it. The Ninja Foodi is therefore Ninja Foodi is not difficult to operate.

5. It will Replace the Counter Space of 2 Kitchen Appliances.

This kitchen unit can perform the function of both Instant Pot and Air Fryer. This means you can pressure cook your food and equally crisp it. This can be possible when you are cooking chicken that you can pressure cook so its tender and then tender crisp it so that the skin gets crispy. For the fact that this appliance can perform the function of both Instant Pot and Air Fryer, it saves space in your kitchen if you were to buy both Instant Pot and Air Fryer.

6. The User Interface is Easy to Understand.

Some pressure cookers will require new users to thorough tutorials on how to operate the unit. Ninja Foodi display unit and buttons are very easy to understand without the help of a tutor. You can learn how to cook 2 different foods at the same time.

7. It is Very Easy to Clean.

Cleaning the Ninja Foodi is not cumbersome. You just need to get a warm soapy water with a rack cloth to clean both the internal and external body parts.

Function Buttons of Your Ninja Foodi

1. **Pressure Cooker:**

This button is used to set the temperature. You can set it high or low and you can also customize the cooking time up to 4 hours. When using this button, make sure that the black valve on the top of the Ninja Foodi is set to seal position.

2. **Dehydration:**

This button is only on certain models and is used with the crisping lid on. It enables you to adjust temperature from 105° F to 195° F with a cooking time adjustment from 15 minutes up to 12 hours. Note that fruits and vegetables should be patted as dry as possible before arranging them in the cook and crisp basket. The longer you dehydrate ingredients, the crispier they will get.

3. **Keep Warm:**

This button can be used on its own to keep your ingredients at a food-safe temperature and it works perfectly for items that are cooked in the Ninja Foodi.

4. **Steam:**

If you are using this button, there's no temperature adjustment. You can adjust the cooking time to about 30 minutes. You must make sure that you set the black valve on the top of the Ninja Foodi to vent position, not seal position.

5. **Slow Cook:**

This button is similar to the normal slow cooker while can enable you to set the cooking time up to 12 hours. You can set it to slow cook high or slow cook low. The slow cook mode requires that you set the black valve on the top of the Ninja Foodi is set to vent not seal position.

6. **Sear/Sauté:**

This function does not give you opportunity to set the time but it has different temperature modes which includes high, medium high, medium, low and medium low etc. Since you cannot set the time, it stays until it goes off. Use LO for simmering, MED for sautéing, and HI for boiling or searing meats. When searing meats, keep them out at room temperature for 20–30 minutes, and pat dry before searing I'm order to give you a better result.

7. **Air Crisp:**

This function enables you to set the time upto 1 hour and also adjust the temperature 300° F to 400° F. It helps you to cook chicken and make the skin crispy.

8. **Bake / Roast:**

This button enables you to bake and roast food and make it delicious. For instance, if you want to cook roasted chicken or cake, this button will help you to get a better result. It has temperature settings from 250° F up to 400° F and you can customize the time up to 4 hours.

9. **Broil:**

This mode doesn't have temperature adjustment. It is either you switch it on or you switch it off. You can adjust the cooking time to about 30 minutes.

The Broil Function does not have a temperature adjustment, it is either on or off. You can adjust the time up to 30 minutes.

Ninja Foodi Pressure Releasing Method

Using this button sometimes can be a little bit intimidating to beginners who are new to Pressure Releasing Method. Using the quick pressure release is more intimidating than using the natural pressure release. However it is very simple and easy when you get to know it. Immediately the cook cycle ends, your pressure cooker will beep. At this point, the recipe will direct you to release the pressure in the cooking pot. You can release the pressure either by quick pressure release or a natural pressure release.

This is how to use a quick pressure release: Turn the pressure release switch to the Venting position and let the steam to release quickly when the cooking cycle is over. You will see a strong jet of steam coming from the pressure release valve. In case you see drops of liquid coming out from the pressure release valve, you just need to switch the valve back to the Sealed position and use an Intermittent Pressure Release. For safety reasons, please keep your face away from the steam while doing a quick pressure release.

However, this is how to use a natural pressure release: Keep the pressure release switch in the sealed position when the cook cycle is over. The pressure will now be released slowly, without you doing anything. Immediately the pressure is fully released, the float valve will drop and the lid will unlock and open by itself.

Please note that while doing a natural pressure release, the cooking continues so you need to take that in to account when determining your cooking time.

Steps to Use Your Ninja Foodi

1. **Make sure you use at least ½ or 1 cup liquid in the inner pot when pressure-cooking.**

Ninja Foodi inner pot requires that you put at least ½ to 1 cup of liquid in order to help the appliance come to Pressure. If you put too much water, the appliance will also take a longer time to come to Pressure and also take longer time to release pressure when the cooking cycle is over.

2. **Try to use different buttons in a cooking session.**

Ninja Foodi enables you to cook the whole food in the same inner pot. You can begin to brown the meat, onions or garlic using the sauté button. Put the rest of the ingredients into the pot and pressure cook. When the cooking cycle is over, you can use the pressure release button and then you select the keep warm button in order to keep the food warm until you are ready to serve the food to your family.

3. **Always add extra 10-20 minutes to listed cooking time.**

Pressure cookers always take about 10 minutes to come to Pressure before they begin the normal cooking time. Some cookbook authors do not add the preheating time to the cooking time so you need to add this preheating time to the recipe's cooking time. For instance if the recipe calls for 20 minutes cooking time, you are going to add extra 10 minutes to make it 30 minutes. At the end of the cooking cycle, you also need to add another 5 or 10 minutes in order to release pressure from the unit.

4. **Carryout regular safety checks on your Ninja Foodi.**

It is advisable to check for safety of your appliance regularly. Any electronic products may develop fault anytime and any day. Always check your unit to know if it is in good condition before you commence cooking. If you develop the habit of checking your appliance regularly, you are guaranteed of using the appliance for a long period of time. Replace any body parts you found that is faulty. Do not manage it when you notice any fault. Always make sure your vent are clean regularly.

Useful Tips for Using Your Ninja Foodi

The Ninja Foodi was programmed to perform both the function of Air Fryer and Instant Pot. This is what makes the Ninja Foodi to be unique. The Ninja Foodi has the capacity to do many things. It can cook frozen fries, and cake. It can also grill, broil, stir fry and roast. The Ninja Foodi is very easy to operate. You can equally steam, sauté, warm, stew, and make yogurt just like the Instant Pot.

The digital control panel is not cumbersome to read and use, it is very simple. There are different buttons that are dedicated to perform functions like adjusting the cooking time and temperature. Ninja Foodi was not programed to have a specific settings for a particular food unlike other pressure cookers have.

Ninja Foodi comes with 2 lids. One lid is for Air-frying, crisping and Dehydrating while the other lid is for pressure cooking. The crisping lid is large and permanently attached to the unit which makes it a bit clunky and difficult to store in a cabinet. The Tender-crisp feature allows you to quickly cook ingredients and then make use of the Crisping Lid for a perfect finish.

The Instant Pot cannot do this. The Ninja Foodi cooks faster than the traditional cooking method by about 70%. The Ninja Foodi cooking pot and basket is ceramic coated and nonstick, which makes it easy to clean. In addition to the basket, two lids and cooking pot, Ninja Foodi's manufacturer also provides a stainless steel reversible rack and a recipe cookbook about 50 free recipes. Ninja Foodi body parts are all dishwasher-safe. The unit is nonstick and very easy to clean. Make sure you clean the unit after every use.

Ninja Foodi Trouble Shooting

1. **My Ninja Foodi does not power on.**

The unit will not turn on when you press the power button. This could be as a result of improper plugging of the power cord. The Ninja Foodi has two power cords that needs to be firmly plugged into the wall socket. Confirm that the cords are firmly plugged in the wall socket.

2. **The Ninja Foodi cooking Basket is improperly installed.**

The Ninja Foodi is programmed in such a way that if the cooking basket is wrongly placed, the unit will not switch on even when the power button is pressed. To resolve this, simply remove the cooking basket and put it back and endure it is properly fixed.

3. **Timer does not function properly.**

Timer does not pop up on the display window when pressed. It could be that the timer button is broken. If the unit is plugged already to power source, unplug and replug it. The timer should work now but if it doesn't work, press and hold the up arrow on the temperature to try and restart the timer. Make sure that the timer is working and just not setting, and make sure you press start to begin the timer. Check also that the basket is in, allowing you to set and adjust the time.

4. **The Ninja Foodi controls are not working.**

If your unit is on standby, hit the power button to turn the unit back on. If the Ninja Foodi is in standby mode, the controls may not respond.

5. The Ninja Foodi is powered on, but will not heat up to cook.

This could be as a result of no time for the unit to Preheat and come to Pressure. The Ninja Foodi needs time to preheat before reaching the set cooking temperature. The unit must reach the accurate temperature before you begin to cook your food.

6. **My food didn't cook.**

Check well, it could be that the cooking basket is not properly fixed to the unit. To get a better result, make sure the ingredients are arranged equally in a layer in the bottom of the cooking basket and avoid overcrowding. Select the up and down buttons to adjust the time and temperature.

Ninja Foodi Frequently Asked Questions and Answers

1. **How Does the Ninja Foodi Work as an Air Fryer and Pressure Cooker?**

The Ninja Foodi was programmed to perform both the function of Air Fryer and Instant Pot. This is what makes the Ninja Foodi to be unique. The appliance has Air Fryer lid that stays on but open to the side while pressure cooking. The pressure cooker lid that has venting and seal capability is pop on when using the pressure cooker mode. Ninja Foodi also come with the wire trivet which enables you to cook more than one food at the same time. For instance you can cook vegetables and meat at the same time. In order to use the Ninja Foodi as an Air Fryer you need to place the Air Fryer cooking basket and close the permanent lid.

2. **How Do I Choose the Right Time for Pressure Cooking?**

When selecting the cooking time, you must consider how voluminous the food is. Note that you must include the time that the unit will take before if come to Pressure. If cook time was 30 minutes, you have to select 40 minutes as your cooking time.

3. **How Much Liquid Should I Use When Pressure cooking?**

There's no fixed amount of water that you can use when pressure-cooking. However, some water and not suitable to create steam that's required for Pressure cooking. You can use liquid like milk, cream-based soups, and tomato sauce but you will need to add thinner liquid to enable the unit come to Pressure.

4. **Should I Use The Basket or Rack When Air Frying?**

The cooking basket that comes with the unit is meant to be used with the Air Fryer, steam or bake function. Always ensure you use the basket with the diverter in order to enable air to circulate under the cooking basket to help brown the bottom of the food.

5. **How Can I Convert Instant Pot Recipes for the Ninja Foodi?**

The Ninja Foodi can also perform Instant Pot function. So it is possible to convert from Instant Pot recipes to Ninja Foodi recipes. Instant Pot recipes are written using the High or Low pressure settings and can be easily converted to the Ninja Foodi's pressure cooking function by following the same instructions. Note that if a recipe does not specify High or Low setting for pressure cooking, assume it is high.

6. Can I use Aluminum Foil in the Ninja Foodi for Air Fryer vegetables?

The answer is absolutely yes!!! It is possible to use Aluminum foil in the Ninja Foodi for Air Fryer vegetables. You need to note that you need to be sure the foil is rolled up on the side so that air is still able to circulate.

7. Can I Cook Frozen Vegetables in the Ninja Foodi?

The answer is absolutely yes!!! It is possible and easy to cook frozen vegetables in the Ninja Foodi. You need to add a nice and suitable cooking spray and a pinch of salt. You will have to use the Air crisp function. Cooking frozen vegetables in the Ninja Foodi will take the same cooking time as That of regular raw vegetables.

8. What Type of Ninja Foodi Vegetable Recipes Can I Cook?

There are no specific vegetables that can only be cooked in the Ninja Foodi. This means you can cook any kinds of vegetables in the Ninja Foodi. It tastes so delicious.

NINJA FOODI BREAKFAST RECIPES

Pretzel Bites

Preparation Time: 20 minutes

Cook Time: 5 minutes

Total Time: 25 minutes

Serves: 8

Calories: 228 kcal

Ingredients:

- 4 Cups of boiling water
- ⅓ Cup of baking soda
- 1 Package of active dry yeast
- 3 Cups of all-purpose flour
- ½ Cup of warm water
- 1 Tbsp. brown sugar
- 1 Tsp. salt
- 1 Tbsp. coarse salt
- 4 Tbsp. butter melted

Cooking Instructions:

1. Put the yeast in a bowl of water and keep it to dissolve. Put brown sugar and salt. Mix well. Measure one cup of flour and add to the bowl.

2. Repeat this and make sure the dough is sticky. Keep the dough for at least 10 minutes. Place the dough in a cutting board already spread with flour.

3. Cut the dough to about 8 pieces equally. Roll each dough into a snake shape. Boil 4 cups of water and baking soda, dump in 10 pieces of the dough and remove after 20 seconds.

4. Lay the pieces on a baking sheet lined with parchment paper and spray salt on top. Set your Ninja Foodi to Oven setting. Select to cook at 390°F for 5 minutes.

5. Close the lid and press start button. Lay the dough into the Ninja Foodi and cook. When the cooking cycle is over, remove the dough and brush with melted butter.

6. Serve and enjoy!!!

Hash Brown Casserole

Preparation Time: 5 minutes

Cook Time: 30 minutes

Total Time: 35 minutes

Serves: 12

Calories: 238 kcal

Ingredients:

- 1 Lb. Ham
- ½ Cup of cheddar cheese
- 6 Eggs
- 48 Oz. bag frozen hash browns
- ¼ Cup of milk
- 1 Large onion
- 3 Tbsp. olive oil

Cooking Instructions:

1. Hit the sauté button on your Ninja Foodi. Dump in onions and olive oil and then sauté to your desired consistency. Dump in the hash browns.

2. Set the Ninja Foodi to cook at 350°F for 15 minutes. When the cooking cycle elapses, combine together milk and eggs. Apply the mixture on the hash browns.

3. Lay the meat on the top. Set the Ninja Foodi again to cook at 350°F for 10 minutes. Spread cheddar cheese on the top.

4. Serve and enjoy!!!

French Toast Casserole

Preparation Time: 5 minutes

Cook Time: 20 minutes

Total Time: 25 minutes

Serves: 6

Calories: 140 kcal

Ingredients:

- 2 Tbs. milk
- 1 Tbs. cinnamon
- 2 Packs of Grands cinnamon rolls
- 4 Eggs
- 1 Tbs. vanilla

Cooking Instructions:

1. Merge together vanilla, milk and eggs in a small mixing bowl. Open the cinnamon rolls and cut the dough into 4 pieces.

2. Spray the Ninja Foodi basket with cooking oil. Keep the dough in the pan and spread the egg mixture on the pan.

3. Bake the dough at 300°F for 20 minutes. When the cooking cycle is over, remove the dough and top with syrup.

4. Serve and enjoy!!!

Apple Pie Monkey Bread Muffins

Preparation Time: 5 minutes

Cook Time: 14 minutes

Total Time: 19 minutes

Serves: 12

Calories: 52 kcal

Ingredients:

- 10 Cinnamon rolls
- 1 Can of apple pie filling

Cooking Instructions:

1. Divide the cinnamon rolls into 9 places into a small mixing bowl and add pie filling. Cut the larger pieces of apple into smaller pieces and stir well.

2. Spray a muffin tin well with nonstick spray. Scoop the Apple mixture into muffin tin holes.

3. Set the Ninja Foodi to cook at 350°F for 20 minutes. When the cooking cycle elapses, remove from heat and allow it to cool for about 5 minutes.

4. Serve and enjoy!!!

Cookies

Preparation Time: 15 minutes

Cook Time: 8 minutes

Total Time: 23 minutes

Serves: 18

Calories: 172 kcal

Ingredients:

- 1 Tsp. baking soda
- 1 Cup of chocolate chips
- ½ Cup of butter
- ¼ Cup of sugar
- ½ Cup of brown sugar
- 1 Egg
- 1 ½ Tsp. vanilla
- 1 ½ Cup of all-purpose flour
- ½ Tsp. salt

Cooking Instructions:

1. Begin by combining together butter, sugar, egg, vanilla and brown sugar in a small mixing bowl.

2. In another small mixing bowl merge together salt, baking soda and flour. Give it a nice mix and pour it into the egg mixture.

3. Fold in chips. Use spoon to fold in chips. Put a piece of parchment paper into basket and scoop the mixture into the Ninja Foodi making sure the sizes are equal.

4. Set the Ninja Foodi to cook at 300°F for 8 minutes. When the cooking cycle is over, remove and keep the cookies and allow it to cool.

5. Serve and enjoy!!!

Pot Roast

Preparation Time: 10 minutes

Cook Time: 1 hour

Total Time: 1 hour 10 minutes

Serves: 8

Calories: 361 kcal

Ingredients:

- ¼ Cup of water cold
- 2 Tbsp. cornstarch
- 3 Lbs. beef roast
- 2 Tbsp. olive oil
- 1 Tsp. salt
- ½ Tsp. pepper
- 1 Tsp. garlic powder
- 1 Tsp. onion powder
- 1 Onion sliced
- 4 Cups of beef broth
- Gravy

Cooking Instructions:

1. Begin by applying salt, garlic powder, pepper and onion on all sides of the roast. Hit sauté button on the Ninja Foodi and put small oil.

2. Put the roast and sauté to your desired consistency. Dump in beef broth and onions to the pot. Lock the lid and set on the Ninja Foodi on high pressure to cook for an hour. 60 minutes.

3. When the cooking time is up, do a quick pressure release for 10 minutes. Remove roast and onions. In a small bowl, merge together cold water and cornstarch.

4. Hit sauté button on the Ninja Foodi. When the juice begins to boil, slowly put this mixture. Cook to your desired consistency.

5. Serve and enjoy!!!

Oatmeal

Preparation Time: 5 minutes

Cook Time: 5 minutes

Total Time: 10 minutes

Serves: 4

Calories: 192 kcal

Ingredients:

- 3 Tbsp. butter
- Pinch of cinnamon
- 1 Cup of oats
- 2 ½ Cups of water
- 1 Cup of apple skinned and diced
- 2 Tbsp. brown sugar

Cooking Instructions:

1. Keep the Ninja Foodi on sauté mode. Put butter and melt it.

2. Dump in oats, brown sugar, water and cinnamon. Stir properly.

3. Set the Ninja Foodi to cook at 300°F for 5 minutes. When the cooking cycle is over, remove and switch off the Ninja Foodi.

4. Serve and enjoy!!!

Homemade Bread

Preparation Time: 10 minutes

Cook Time: 30 minutes

Total Time: 40 minutes

Serves: 12

Calories: 129 kcal

Ingredients:

- 2 ¼ Tsp. active dry yeast
- 1 Tbsp. olive oil
- 3 Cups of all-purpose flour
- 1 Cup of warm water
- 1 Tsp. sea salt
- 2 Tsp. white sugar

Cooking Instructions:

1. Merge together yeast, sugar and warm water (1 Tsp.) into a small mixing bowl. Stir properly and keep it for at least 5 minutes.

2. In a separate medium mixing bowl, merge together salt, 3 cups of flour and the yeast mixture. Stir well and add water to your desired consistency.

3. Turn the mixture out on a floured surface. Start to knead, bringing in the loose flour with each turn for about 15 minutes.

4. Put 1 Tbsp. of Olive oil to the inner pot of the Ninja Foodi. Cover the top of the dough ball with olive oil and put them into the inner pot.

5. Use a damp towel to cover it. Cook in the Ninja Foodi at 105° F for 30 minutes. Get the dough out and punch down.

6. Make into the shape of the bread round you want and replace in the Ninja Foodi. Cover with damp towel and cook at 105° F for 30 minutes.

7. Remove the dough and make a 3 straight line on the top. Use bake mode and bake at 325° F for 30 minutes.

8. Serve and enjoy!!!

Frozen Egg Rolls

Preparation Time: 5 minutes

Cook Time: 10 minutes

Total Time: 15 minutes

Serves: 4

Calories: 137 kcal

Ingredients:

- 4 Egg rolls frozen

Cooking Instructions:

1. Lay the frozen egg rolls in the inner pot of the Ninja Foodi and cook for 10 minutes.

2. When the cooking cycle is over, remove the egg and allow it to cool for at least 5 minutes.

3. Serve and enjoy!!!

Green Tomatoes

Preparation Time: 15 minutes

Cook Time: 8 minutes

Total Time: 23 minutes

Serves: 8

Calories: 69 kcal

Ingredients:

- Salt to taste
- Pepper to taste
- 2 Green tomatoes sliced
- 1 Cup of pork rinds crushed
- ½ Cup of flour
- 1 Egg beaten
- 1 Tbsp. heavy whipping cream
- ¼ Tsp. paprika

Cooking Instructions:

1. In a small mixing bowl, merge together flour, salt, pepper and paprika. In another small mixing bowl, mix together the egg and heavy cream. Slice the tomatoes.

2. Put crushed pork rinds in a separate small mixing bowl. Coat each tomato slice with the flour mixture, egg mixture and Pork rinds respectively.

3. Place them in the inner pot of the Ninja Foodi. Set the Ninja Foodi to cook at 105° F for 30 minutes.

4. Serve and enjoy!!!

Sausage

Preparation Time: 5 minutes

Cook Time: 13 minutes

Total Time: 18 minutes

Serves: 6

Calories: 258 kcal

Ingredients:

- 6 Sausage
- Olive oil spray
- 1 ½ Cup of water

Cooking Instructions:

1. Put the water into the Ninja Foodi. Lay air fryer basket inside pot and spray with nonstick cooking spray.

2. Put sausage links inside. Close pressure cooker lid and steam valve and set to cook at high pressure for 5 minutes. Do Quick pressure release when done and remove lid.

3. Spray links with olive oil and lock the air crisp lid. Set to cook at 400°F for 8 minutes.

4. Serve and enjoy!!!

Pumpkin Zucchini Muffins

Preparation Time: 15 minutes

Cook Time: 20 minutes

Total Time: 35 minutes

Serves: 18

Calories: 336 kcal

Ingredients:

- ½ Tsp. cinnamon
- ½ Tsp. nutmeg
- 1 Cup of pumpkin canned
- 3 Eggs
- 2 Cup of sugar
- 1 Cup of butter melted
- 2 Cup of zucchini shredded
- 3 Cup of flour all purpose
- 1 Tsp. baking soda
- ½ Tsp. baking powder

Cooking Instructions:

1. Blend together butter, pumpkin, eggs and sugar in a food processor. In a small mixing bowl, merge together the flour, baking soda and baking powder. Mix well.

2. Pour this dry mixture into the food blender mixture and blend to your desired consistency. Add Shredded zucchini and nutmeg. Give it a good mix.

3. Put the mixture into Muffins and lay them in the inner pot of Ninja Foodi. Set the Ninja Foodi to cook at 300°F for 20 minutes. Serve and enjoy!!!

Sweet Potato Breakfast Hash

Preparation Time: 5 minutes

Cook Time: 15 minutes

Total Time: 20 minutes

Serves: 1

Calories: 185 kcal

Ingredients:

- ¼ Cup of basil
- ¼ Tsp. of salt
- 2 Cups of chopped potatoes
- 1 Cup of chopped onion
- ¼ Cup of garlic puree
- ¼ Cup of olive oil
- ¼ Cup of vegetable stock
- ¼ Cup of rosemary

Cooking Instructions:

1. Put onion, Garlic, and olive oil into the Ninja Foodi and sauté pressing the sauté button. Add potatoes and vegetable stock. Give it a good stir.

2. Hit the broil button on the Ninja Foodi and set on high to cook for 5 minutes. When the cooking cycle is over, open the lid and allow the content to cool off.

3. Add Rosemary, basil and salt. Give it a good stir.

4. Serve and enjoy!!!

Scrambled Eggs

Preparation Time: 10 minutes

Cook Time: 11 minutes

Total Time: 21 minutes

Serves: 6

Calories: 294 kcal

Ingredients:

- ¾ Cup of cheese shredded
- ½ Lb. sausage (spicy)
- ¾ Cup of onion diced
- 1 Tbsp. olive oil
- 5 Mushrooms sliced
- 8 Eggs scrambled
- ¼ Cup of cream of mushroom soup
- ½ Tsp. garlic salt

Cooking Instructions:

1. Hit sauté button on the Ninja Foodi. Put oil, diced onions, mushroom and sausage. Sauté to your desired consistency.

2. Beat the egg into a small mixing bowl, mix well and pour into the Ninja Foodi alongside with your meat.

3. Add garlic, salt, ½ cup of shredded cheese, and add 1/4 cup of cream of mushroom soup. Stir properly.

4. Put the mixture into the Ninja Foodi inner pot and set to cook at 390°F for 5 minutes.

5. Open the lid and check for doneness. Lock the lid again and see to air crisp at 390°F for 6 minutes. Top with cheese and chives.

6. Serve and enjoy!!!

NINJA FOODI POULTRY RECIPES

Asian Shredded Chicken

Preparation Time: 5 minutes

Cook Time: 15 minutes

Total Time: 20 minutes

Serves: 4

Calories: 162 kcal

Ingredients:

- 1 Tbsp. lemongrass paste
- 1 Tbsp. chili garlic sauce
- 1 Lb. chicken breast frozen
- 1 Tbsp. soy sauce
- 1 Cup of chicken stock
- 2 Tsp. fish sauce
- ¼ Tsp. sea salt fine grind
- ¼ Tsp. black pepper
- 2 Tbsp. rice vinegar

Cooking Instructions:

1. Put chicken and all the rest of the ingredients to the inner pot of the Ninja Foodi. Close the lid and set the Ninja Foodi to cook at 370°F at 15 minutes.

2. When cooking cycle is over, do natural pressure release for 10 minutes. Use two forks and shred the chicken.

3. Serve and enjoy!!!

Buffalo Chicken Wings

Preparation Time: 10 minutes

Cook Time: 20 minutes

Total Time: 30 minutes

Serves: 4

Calories: 242 kcal

Ingredients:

- ½ Cup of water
- 2 Lb. frozen chicken wings
- 2 Tbsp. canola oil
- 2 Tbsp. Buffalo sauce
- 2 Tsp. kosher salt

Cooking Instructions:

1. Fill the Ninja Foodi pot with the water, keep the chicken wings in the basket and lay the basket in the pot.

2. Close the lid and set the Ninja Foodi to cook at 370°F at 5 minutes. When cooking cycle is over, do natural pressure release for 10 minutes.

3. Pat wings dry using paper towels and toss with 2 Tbsp. oil in the basket. Lock the crisping lid. Hit Air Crisp button and set to cook at 390°F for 15 minutes.

4. When cooking is completely done, stir together Buffalo Sauce and salt in a large mixing bowl and then dump the wings into the buffalo mixture. Toss well.

5. Serve and enjoy!!!

Root Beer Chicken Wings

Preparation Time: 10 minutes

Cook Time: 18 minutes

Total Time: 28 minutes

Serves: 2

Calories: 188 kcal

Ingredients:

- 2 Lbs. of chicken wings
- 1 Can of root beer
- ¼ Cup of brown sugar
- ¼ Cup of root beer

Cooking Instructions:

1. Put the chicken wings into the inner pot of the Ninja Foodi. Add the root beer and close the Ninja Foodi lid.

2. Close the lid and set the Ninja Foodi to cook at 370°F at 18 minutes. When cooking cycle is over, do natural pressure release for 10 minutes.

3. Remove the wings. Combine together brown sugar and soda in a small mixing bowl. Brush the mixture on the chicken wings.

4. Lock the crisping lid. Hit AIR CRISP button and set to cook at 390°F for 2 minutes. Serve and enjoy!!!

Chicken Satay

Preparation Time: 10 minutes

Cook Time: 6 minutes

Total Time: 16 minutes

Serves: 6

Calories: 177 kcal

Ingredients:

- 1½ Lbs. chicken breast boneless, skinless

Marinade:

- Chopped peanuts
- Peanut sauce
- ½ Cup of coconut milk
- 2 Cloves of garlic, minced
- 2" Piece of ginger, grated
- 2 Tsp. turmeric
- 1 Tsp. sea salt fine grind
- 1 Tbsp. Lemongrass Paste
- 1 Tbsp. Chili Garlic Sauce
- 2 Tsp. Lemon Juice
- Chopped cilantro

Cooking Instructions:

1. Combine together all the ingredients in the marinade in a medium mixing bowl. Cut the chicken breast into ½" strips. Add it to the marinade mixture.

2. Close and keep it for 30 minutes. Turn the Ninja Foodi grill on and hit the Grill button. Preheat the Ninja Foodi to 380°F.

3. While the Ninja Foodi preheats, gather your chicken skewers. Take a strip and weave it onto a skewer. You can fit multiple on a skewer.

4. Make sure the chicken is not bunched. Continue until you use all the chicken. Add about 6 skewers to the grilling surface.

5. Close the lid and set to cook for 6 minutes. Cook for 3 minutes and flip the skewers. Cook an additional 3 minutes.

6. Garnish with fresh cilantro and chopped peanuts.

7. Serve and enjoy!!!

Buffalo and Ranch Wings

Preparation Time: 1 minute

Cook Time: 12 minutes

Total Time: 13 minutes

Serve: 4

Calories: 447 kcal

Ingredients:

- ½ Cup of water
- 1 Stick butter melted
- 3 Lbs. frozen chicken wings
- 1 Packet of ranch seasoning
- 1 Cup of hot sauce

Cooking Instructions:

1. Arrange the chicken wings in the inner pot of the Ninja Foodi. Merge together the butter, ranch packet and hot sauce.

2. Pour the mixture into the pot to properly coat the chicken wings. Add the water and Close the lid and set to cook for 12 minutes.

3. Put wings on a baking sheet and put in broiler for 2 minutes.

4. Serve and enjoy!!!

Chicken Enchiladas

Preparation Time: 10 minutes

Cook Time: 30 minutes

Total Time: 40 minutes

Serve: 6

Calories: 331 kcal

Ingredients:

- 12 Corn tortillas
- 1½ Cups of Mexican Shredded Chicken
- 2 Cups of Enchilada Sauce
- 1½ Cups of Mexican Shredded Cheese

Cooking Instructions:

1. Begin by spritzing 6 corn tortillas with oil and line the basket of the Ninja Foodi basket with the tortillas. Cook in the Ninja Foodi at 425°F for 5 minutes.

2. Repeat with remaining 6 corn tortillas. Put 3 Tbsp. of filling to each corn tortilla, roll and place in pairs on non-stick tray.

3. Scoop about ⅓ cup of enchilada sauce and spread on the tops of each pair. Place the tray in the Ninja Foodi and bake at 325°F for 20 minutes.

4. Put about ¼ cup of Mexican Shredded Cheese to the top of each pair and replace them back to the pot. Cook on high for 3 minutes. Top with your favorite toppings.

5. Serve and enjoy!!!

Mexican Shredded Chicken

Preparation Time: 5 minutes

Cook Time: 25 minutes

Total Time: 30 minutes

Serve: 6

Calories: 171 kcal

Ingredients:

- 1 Bunch of cilantro stems
- 1½ Lbs. chicken breasts, frozen
- 14 ½ Oz. Fire Roasted Tomatoes
- 1 Cup of chicken stock
- ½ Onion
- 1 Jalapeno pepper
- 2 Tsp. sea salt
- 2 Tsp. cumin
- 1 Tsp. garlic powder
- 1 Tsp. onion powder

Cooking Instructions:

1. Begin by mixing together the chicken stock, roasted tomatoes, onion, sliced jalapeno pepper, and spices to the inner pot of the Ninja Foodi and stir thoroughly.

2. Trim out the stems of 1 bunch of cilantro and cut into about ½" size and add to the pot. Remain the cilantro leaves for garnish.

3. Arrange the chicken breasts into the pot. Put the pressure lid on and be sure the valve is in seal position. Select high pressure and set to cook for 25 minutes.

4. When the cooking cycle is up, allow the pot to natural release the pressure for 10 minutes. Shred the chicken with two forks.

5. Serve and enjoy!!!

Jalapeno Hot Popper and Chicken Dip

Preparation Time: 3 minutes

Cook Time: 12 minutes

Total Time: 15 minutes

Serve: 4

Calories: 309 kcal

Ingredients:

- 1 Lb. boneless chicken breast
- 8 Oz. cream cheese
- 3 Jalapenos, sliced
- 8 Oz. cheddar cheese
- ¾ Cup of sour cream
- ½ Cup of panko bread crumbs
- ½ Cup of water

Cooking Instructions:

1. Arrange chicken breast, Jalapenos, cream cheese and water in the inner pot of Ninja Foodi.

2. Put the pressure lid on and be sure the valve is in seal position. Select high pressure and set to cook for 12 minutes.

3. When the cooking cycle is up, allow the pot to natural release the pressure for 10 minutes. Open the pot and shred the chicken with two forks.

4. Put 6 Oz. cheddar cheese and sour cream. Put in the Ninja Foodi and cook for 3 minutes. Serve and enjoy!!!

Crack Chicken

Preparation Time: 5 minutes

Cook Time: 15 minutes

Total Time: 20 minutes

Serve: 4

Calories: 165 kcal

Ingredients:

- ½ Cup of water
- 1 Cup of cheddar cheese
- 6 Slices of cooked bacon
- 2 Lbs. boneless chicken breast
- 1 Packet of ranch seasoning
- 8 Oz. cream cheese

Cooking Instructions:

1. Arrange the chicken and cream cheese in the inner pot of the Ninja Foodi. Dump in ranch seasoning and water.

2. Put the pressure lid on and be sure the valve is in seal position. Select high pressure and set to cook for 15 minutes.

3. When the cooking cycle is up, do quick pressure release for 10 minutes. Open the pot and shred the chicken with two forks.

4. Add the chicken back to Ninja Foodi and stir in cheese and bacon.

5. Serve and enjoy!!!

Cracked up Tator Tots with Chicken

Preparation Time: 2 minutes

Cook Time: 20 minutes

Total Time: 22 minutes

Serve: 4

Calories: 365 kcal

Ingredients:

- 1 Packet of ranch seasoning
- 1 Cup of water
- 2 Chicken breasts
- 1 Bag of frozen tater tots, cooked according to package
- 16 Oz. cheddar cheese
- 6 Slices of cooked bacon

Cooking Instructions:

1. Arrange tater tots and bacon in the inner pot of the Ninja Foodi and cook to your desired consistency. Remove and set aside.

2. Put the chicken breast in the Ninja Foodi with one cup water alongside with ranch seasoning. Put the pressure lid on and be sure the valve is in seal position.

3. Select high pressure and set to cook for 12 minutes. When the cooking cycle is up, do quick pressure release for 10 minutes.

4. Open the pot and shred the chicken with two forks. Combine together chicken, tater tots, bacon and cheese. Cook for about 5 minutes.

5. Serve and enjoy!!!

30 Minutes Fall Off the Bone Ribs

Preparation Time: 10 minutes

Cook Time: 25 minutes

Total Time: 35 minutes

Serve: 2

Calories: 195 kcal

Ingredients:

- 2 Racks of ribs
- 2 Cups of apple juice
- 1 Coors Light Beer
- 1 Cup of BBQ Sauce

Cooking Instructions:

1. Put apple juice and beer into the Ninja Foodi inner pot. Add ribs (the meat side should be down).

2. Put the pressure lid on and be sure the valve is in seal position. Select high pressure and set to cook for 25 minutes.

3. When the cooking cycle is up, do a quick pressure release for 10 minutes. Remove Ribs and pour BBQ sauce on top of the ribs.

4. Serve and enjoy!!!

NINJA FOODI BEEF & PORK RECIPES

Tender BBQ Ribs

Preparation Time: 10 minutes

Cook Time: 25 minutes

Total Time: 35 minutes

Serve: 8

Calories: 324 kcal

Ingredients:

- 1 Tsp. garlic salt
- 1 Rack of pork ribs, membrane removed
- 6 Cups of apple juice
- ¼ Cup of brown sugar
- 1 Tbsp. salt

Cooking Instructions:

1. Lay the ribs in the inner pot of the Ninja Foodi alongside with apple juice (put enough to submerge).

2. Put the pressure lid on and be sure the valve is in seal position. Select high pressure and set to cook for 25 minutes.

3. When the cooking cycle is up, do a quick pressure release for 10 minutes. Mix together the brown sugar, salt and garlic salt in a small bowl.

4. Pour the mixture on top of the ribs. Put it back to the Ninja Foodi and make it crispy for about 2 minutes.

5. Serve and enjoy!!!

Parmesan Pork Chops

Preparation Time: 10 minutes

Cook Time: 8 minutes

Total Time: 18 minutes

Serve: 2

Calories: 124 kcal

Ingredients:

- 2 Lbs. boneless pork chops
- 1 Cup of Italian style bread crumbs
- ½ Cup of grated parmesan cheese
- 1 Tbsp. Italian seasoning
- 2 Eggs
- Olive oil

Cooking Instructions:

1. Set the Ninja Foodi to stovetop high. Put enough oil to cover the bottom of the Ninja Foodi inner pot. Beat the eggs into a small mixing bowl.

2. Add the bread crumbs, seasonings and grated cheese into a Ziploc bag. Tight the bag completely. Shake the bag well.

3. Bury each pork chop into the egg, then place it into the baggie and shake to coat thoroughly. Arrange the pork chops into the Ninja Foodi.

4. Put the pressure lid on and be sure the valve is in seal position. Select high pressure and set to cook for 8 minutes.

5. When the cooking cycle is up, do quick pressure release for 10 minutes. Top with your favorite side.

6. Serve and enjoy!!!

Bacon Ranch Beef Stroganoff

Preparation Time: 10 minutes

Cook Time: 8 minutes

Total Time: 18 minutes

Serve: 3

Calories: 220 kcal

Ingredients:

- 2 Packets of ranch dressing mix
- 2 Tsp. garlic powder
- 1 ½ Lbs. ground beef
- 1 Lb. egg noodles
- 6 Cups of beef broth
- ¾ Cup of real crumbled bacon
- 16 Oz. sour cream

Cooking Instructions:

1. Add the ground beef and garlic powder into the Ninja Foodi. Select sauté mode and sauté the meat to your desired consistency.

2. Put the noodles and broth to the pot. Put the pressure lid on and be sure the valve is in seal position. Select high pressure and set to cook for 8 minutes.

3. When the cooking cycle is up, do quick pressure release for 10 minutes. Put the bacon, sour cream and ranch mix to the noodles and mix properly.

4. Serve and enjoy!!!

Pork Tenderloin Green Beans

Preparation Time: 10 minutes

Cook Time: 10 minutes

Total Time: 20 minutes

Serve: 1

Calories: 202 kcal

Ingredients:

- 1 Lb. frozen green beans
- 1 ½ Lb. pork tenderloin
- ½ Cups of water

Cooking Instructions:

1. Put water, tenderloin and green beans into the Ninja Foodi. Put the pressure lid on and be sure the valve is in seal position.

2. Select high pressure and set to cook for 8 minutes. When the cooking cycle is up, do quick pressure release for 10 minutes.

3. Serve and enjoy!!!

Italian Beef and Rice

Preparation Time: 10 minutes

Cook Time: 30 minutes

Total Time: 40 minutes

Serve: 4

Calories: 322 kcal

Ingredients:

- 1 Tbsp. Italian seasoning
- 4 Oz. shredded mozzarella cheese
- 1 ½ Lbs. ground beef
- 1 ½ Cups of white rice
- 16 Oz. frozen mixed vegetables
- 2 (14 ¼ Oz.) cans diced tomatoes seasoned with basil, garlic and oregano
- 1 (14 ½ Oz.) can water

Cooking Instructions:

1. Keep the Ninja Foodi in stovetop high mode. Put ground beef and sauté to your desired consistency. Switch the Ninja Foodi to dry oven.

2. Put rice, mixed vegetables, diced tomatoes and water. Put the pressure lid on and be sure the valve is in seal position.

3. Select high pressure and set to cook for 20 minutes. When the cooking cycle is up, do quick pressure release for 10 minutes.

4. Open the lid and give a nice stir. Cook for another 10 minutes. Switch off Ninja Foodi and sprinkle Shredded cheese.

5. Serve and enjoy!!!

Lasagna Shells with Meat Sauce

Preparation Time: 10 minutes

Cook Time: 30 minutes

Total Time: 40 minutes

Serve: 4

Calories: 322 kcal

Ingredients:

- 1 Lb. ground beef
- ¾ Lb. sweet Italian sausage
- 1 Lb. large pasta shells
- 28 Oz. cans tomato sauce
- 2 Tbsp. Italian seasoning
- 3 ½ Cups of water

Cooking Instructions:

1. Keep the Ninja Foodi in stovetop high mode. Put ground beef and sausage links and sauté to your consistency.

2. Remove the sausage links and slice. Put them back to the Ninja Foodi. Add pasta to the pot and then add the tomatoes on top of the pasta.

3. Put seasoning and water. Mix the mixture thoroughly. Put the pressure lid on and be sure the valve is in seal position.

4. Select high pressure and set to cook for 5 minutes. When the cooking cycle is up, do quick pressure release for 10 minutes.

5. Put the ricotta and Shredded Mozzarella to the pot and stir well. Serve and enjoy!!!

Pork Chops

Preparation Time: 10 minutes

Cook Time: 8 minutes

Total Time: 18 minutes

Serve: 4

Calories: 524 kcal

Ingredients:

- 3 Cups of chicken broth
- 2 Bags saffron yellow rice
- 4 Pork chops boneless
- 1 ½ Tsp. salt divided
- ½ Tsp. garlic powder
- ½ Tsp. onion powder
- ¼ Tsp. pepper
- 2 Tbsp. olive oil
- 1 Onion diced

Cooking Instructions:

1. Apply ½ Tsp. Salt, pepper, garlic powder and onion powder on both sides of the pork. Hit sauté button on the Ninja Foodi.

2. Put olive oil, diced onions and pork chops and sauté to your desired consistency. Remove the pork and set aside. Deglaze your pot using the broth.

3. Add uncooked rice and remaining broth. Place trivet on the pot and lay the pork on the top. Put the pressure lid on and be sure the valve is in seal position.

4. Select high pressure and set to cook for 8 minutes. When the cooking cycle is up, do quick pressure release for 10 minutes. Remove pork, plate, and fluff rice in pot.

5. Serve and enjoy!!!

Perfect Roast Beef

Preparation Time: 10 minutes

Cook Time: 1 hour

Total Time: 1 hour 10 minutes

Serve: 6

Calories: 389 kcal

Ingredients:

- 3 Lbs. Top Round Roast

Rub:

- 2 ½ Tsp. onion powder
- 2 ½ Tsp. garlic powder
- 2 Tbsp. sea salt
- 2 Tbsp. pepper course

Cooking Instructions:

1. Mix together the entire rub Ingredients and season the meat with this mixture. Preheat the Ninja Foodi on Broil with the rack inside the inner pot for 10 minutes.

2. Place the roast on the rack and broil for 25 minutes. Put the pressure lid on and be sure the valve is in seal position.

3. Select high pressure and set to cook for 25 minutes. When the cooking cycle is up, do quick pressure release for 10 minutes.

4. Serve and enjoy!!!

Prime Rib

Preparation Time: 5 minutes

Cook Time: 45 minutes

Total Time: 50 minutes

Serve: 6

Calories: 686 kcal

Ingredients:

- 3 Sprigs Rosemary
- ½ Onion sliced
- 3 Lbs. prime rib roast
- 8 Cloves of garlic
- 1 Tbsp. Sea Salt
- ½ Tbsp. pepper

Cooking Instructions:

1. Begin by preheating the Ninja Foodi for 10 minutes. Cut about 6 slits in the fat cap on top. Put garlic cloves in each of the slit.

2. Put sprigs of Rosemary and onion slices on the reversible rack. Add the prime rib roast on top. Place the rack in the Ninja Foodi.

3. Put the pressure lid on and be sure the valve is in seal position. Select high pressure and set to cook for 45 minutes.

4. When the cooking cycle is up, do quick pressure release for 10 minutes. Remove the rack with the prime rib and allow it to cool off.

5. Serve and enjoy!!!

Pulled Pork

Preparation Time: 5 minutes

Cook Time: 25 minutes

Total Time: 30 minutes

Serve: 6

Calories: 289 kcal

Ingredients:

- ¾ Cup of Low Sodium Chicken Broth
- ¾ Cup of BBQ Sauce, divided
- 1 Lb. Pork Tenderloin
- 1 Tbsp. Olive Oil
- ½ Tbsp. Paprika
- ½ Tbsp. Dry Mustard
- 1 Tsp. Kosher Salt
- 1 Tsp. Black Pepper
- ½ Tsp. Cumin
- 1 Tbsp. brown sugar

Cooking Instructions:

1. In a small mixing bowl, combine together the salt, pepper, paprika, dry mustard, cumin, and brown sugar.

2. In another mixing bowl, merge together the chicken broth and ¼ Cup of BBQ Sauce. Brush the pork tenderloin with olive oil.

3. Coat the pork with the first mixture. Keep the Ninja Foodi on sauté mode. Put the pork and sauté for 2 minutes.

4. Turnover and sauté for another 2 minutes and the put the broth mixture. Put the pressure lid on and be sure the valve is in seal position.

5. Select high pressure and set to cook for 12 minutes. When the cooking cycle is up, do quick pressure release for 10 minutes.

6. Remove the cooked pork on to a serving plate.

7. Serve and enjoy!!!

NINJA FOODI FISH & SEAFOOD RECIPES

Coconut Shrimp

Preparation Time: 10 minutes

Cook Time: 6 minutes

Total Time: 16 minutes

Serve: 4

Calories: 100 kcal

Ingredients:

- ¼ Cup of flour all purpose
- Oil
- 8 Large Shrimp
- ½ Cup of sweetened coconut
- ¼ Cup of panko bread crumbs
- 1 Large egg lightly beaten

Cooking Instructions:

1. In a small mixing bowl, merge together the panko and coconut. Beat the egg and put flour into 2 different mixing bowls.

2. Preheat the Ninja Foodi on Broil for 10 minutes. Peel and devein the shrimp, leaving the tail on.

3. Dip the shrimp into the flour, egg, panko and coconut mixture respectively. Spray the basket with oil of your choice and place the shrimp on the bottom of basket.

4. Spray the shrimp again with oil. Put the pressure lid on and be sure the valve is in seal position. Select high pressure and set to cook for 8 minutes.

5. When the cooking cycle is up, do quick pressure release for 10 minutes. Remove the coconut on to a serving plate.

6. Serve and enjoy!!!

Balsamic Shrimp and Sausage

Preparation Time: 5 minutes

Cook Time: 10 minutes

Total Time: 15 minutes

Serve: 4

Calories: 126 kcal

Ingredients:

- 3 Tbsp. balsamic vinegar
- 1 Tsp. brown sugar
- 2 Tbsp. olive oil
- 1 onion
- 1 Green pepper
- 1 Garlic clove, minced
- 8 Jumbo shrimp, peeled and deveined
- 7 Oz. Pecan smoked Andouille sausage
- ½ Tsp. dry basil
- ½ Tsp. oregano
- ½ Tsp. thyme
- ¼ Cup of chicken broth

Cooking Instructions:

1. Set the Ninja Foodi to sauté mode. Put oil, onion and pepper and then sauté to your desired consistency.

2. Put garlic, sausage, shrimp and the remaining ingredients. Put the pressure lid on and be sure the valve is in seal position.

3. Select high pressure and set to cook for 10 minutes. When the cooking cycle is up, do quick pressure release for 10 minutes. Remove the shrimp to a serving plate.

4. Serve and enjoy!!!

Cajun Shrimp

Preparation Time: 15 minutes

Cook Time: 2 minutes

Total Time: 17 minutes

Serve: 6

Calories: 551 kcal

Ingredients:

- 2 Onions quartered
- 3 Ears of corn
- 6 Yukon gold potatoes, quartered
- 1 Jalapeno pepper
- 2 Redchili peppers dried
- 1 Bulb garlic
- 2 Cups of chicken stock
- 14 Oz. Andouille

Sausage:

- 4 Sprigs thyme
- 1 Lemon halved
- 2 Lbs. shrimp, frozen
- 1 Zucchini, halved

Whole Spice Seasoning Blend:

- 1 Tbsp. black peppercorns
- ½ Tbsp. mustard seed
- ½ Tbsp. cumin seed
- 3 Bay leaves
- 2 Tsp. coarse sea salt

- ¼ Tsp. smoked paprika
- ¾ Tsp. garlic powder
- ¼ Tsp. mustard seed
- ½ Tsp. sea salt
- ¼ Tsp. pepper

Cajun Butter:

- ½ Cup. salted butter

Stick:

- ¼ Tsp. smoked paprika
- ⅛ Tsp. chipotle ground

Cooking Instructions:

1. Put the quartered onions in the inner pot of the Ninja Foodi. Trim out the ends of the ears of corn. Put the corn and potatoes into the Ninja Foodi pot.

2. Dump in the whole Spice seasoning blend and add cups of chicken broth. Put one bulb of garlic. Cut the Andouille sausage in ½ lengthwise on the diagonal.

3. Dump into the inner pot alongside with the Thyme and lemon. Pour about ½ cup of water on top of the frozen shrimp and toss with shrimp seasoning.

4. Put into Ninja Foodi inner pot. Add the zucchini. Put the pressure lid on and be sure the valve is in seal position.

5. Select high pressure and set to cook for 2 minutes. When the cooking cycle is up, do quick pressure release for 10 minutes.

6. Melt the Cajun butter and pour over shrimp boil. Serve and Enjoy!!!

Chili Lime Shrimp

Preparation Time: 10 minutes

Cook Time: 3 minutes

Total Time: 14 minutes

Serve: 4

Calories: 257 kcal

Ingredients:

- ¼ Tsp. cumin powder
- ¼ Tsp. cayenne powder
- 16 Oz. shrimp (Frozen, peeled and devein)
- 3 Tbsp. soy sauce
- 1 Tbsp. olive oil
- 2 Tsp. brown sugar
- 1 Tsp. chili powder
- 1 Tsp. lime juice
- ½ Tsp. garlic powder

Cooking Instructions:

1. In a small mixing bowl, merge together the soy sauce, olive oil, brown sugar, chili powder, lime juice, garlic powder, cumin powder, and cayenne powder. Mix well.

2. Dump shrimp into the mixture and stir properly. Keep aside for 15 minutes. Arrange the shrimp in the inner pot of Ninja Foodi.

3. Put the pressure lid on and be sure the valve is in seal position. Select high pressure and set to cook for 3 minutes.

4. When the cooking cycle is up, do quick pressure release for 10 minutes. Remove shrimp onto a serving plate.

5. Serve and enjoy!!!

Salmon Patties

Preparation Time: 5 minutes

Cook Time: 7 minutes

Total Time: 12 minutes

Serve: 2

Calories: 184 kcal

Ingredients:

- 1 Large egg
- 1 Stalk celery, diced
- 7 Oz. canned salmon, drained
- ½ Tsp. Sea salt
- ¼ Tsp. black pepper
- ½ Tsp. Italian seasoning
- ½ Tsp. paprika
- ½ Tsp. onion powder
- ½ Tsp. garlic powder

Cooking Instructions:

1. Place all the ingredients into a medium mixing bowl and give it a good stir. Make the salmon into cakes and lay them on a tray line with parchment paper.

2. Place the salmon in a refrigerator for at least 30 minutes. Preheat the Ninja Foodi on broil for at least 10 minutes.

3. Spray the Ninja Foodi basket with oil. Arrange the salmon on the basket. Put the pressure lid on and be sure the valve is in seal position.

4. Select high pressure and set to cook for 8 minutes. When the cooking cycle is up, do quick pressure release for 10 minutes. Remove the salmon onto a serving plate.

5. Serve and enjoy!!!

Shrimp Boil

Preparation Time: 10 minutes

Cook Time: 5 minutes

Total Time: 15 minutes

Serve: 6

Calories: 322 kcal

Ingredients:

- 1 Lb. red potatoes cut in half
- 4 Ears fresh corn snapped in half
- 12 Oz. Cajun style Andouille sausage, halved
- 4 Cups of water
- 1 ½ Tbsp. Zataran's shrimp boil
- 3 Tsp. Old Bay seasoning divided
- 1 Lb. fresh shrimp peeled and deveined
- 1 Lb. fresh mussels
- ½ Cup of butter melted
- ½ Tsp. garlic powder

Cooking Instructions:

1. Put red potatoes, corn, sausage, water, shrimp boil liquid, and 2 Tsp. old bay into the inner pot of Ninja Foodi. Stir properly.

2. Put the pressure lid on and be sure the valve is in seal position. Select high pressure and set to cook for 4 minutes.

3. When the cooking cycle is up, do quick pressure release for 10 minutes. Open the lid. Add shrimp, mussels and 1 Tsp. of old bay. Stir well and close the lid.

4. Cook on high pressure for a minute. Mix together butter and garlic powder in a small mixing bowl and use as a dipping sauce. Top with parsley and lemon.

5. Serve and enjoy!!!

NINJA FOODI SOUP RECIPES

Corn Chowder

Preparation Time: 10 minutes

Cook Time: 6 hours

Total Time: 6 hours 10 minutes

Serve: 6

Calories: 292 kcal

Ingredients:

- 3 Strips bacon cooked and diced
- ¾ Cup of cheddar cheese, shredded
- 3 Cup of corn kernels frozen
- 1 Small onion diced
- ½ Green pepper diced
- 2 Cup of chicken broth
- 4 Potatoes peeled and diced
- 1 Tsp. salt
- ¼ Tsp. pepper
- 1 Cup of half and half

Cooking Instructions:

1. Set the Ninja Foodi to sauté mode. Dump in corn, onion, green pepper, chicken broth, potatoes, salt and pepper. Sauté to your desired consistency.

2. Carefully put half and half. Put the pressure lid on and be sure the valve is in seal position. Select high pressure and set to cook for 20 minutes.

3. When the cooking cycle is up, do quick pressure release for 10 minutes. Open the lid, flip over on to a serving plate.

4. Top with chopped Bacon and Shredded cheese.

5. Serve and enjoy!!!

French Onion Soup Chicken Bake

Preparation Time: 10 minutes

Cook Time: 23 minutes

Total Time: 33 minutes

Serve: 4

Calories: 280 kcal

Ingredients:

- 2 Tbsp. Garlic, Minced
- 3 Tbsp. olive oil
- 1½ Lbs. Chicken breast
- 2 Medium Onions, sliced
- 10½ Oz. can French onion soup with beef stock
- 11 Slices of Swiss
- Black Pepper

Cooking Instructions:

1. Set the Ninja Foodi to sauté function. Put 1½ Tbsp. Olive oil, onions. Sauté to your desired consistency, remove and keep aside.

2. Season chicken with pepper and put 1 ½ Tbsp. Olive oil into the Ninja Foodi pot. Put garlic and then place chicken on top. Sauté both sides for 2 minutes.

3. Put the cooked onions on top of the chicken breast alongside with a can of water and soup. Put the pressure lid on and be sure the valve is in seal position.

4. Select high pressure and set to cook for 20 minutes. When the cooking cycle is up, do quick pressure release for 10 minutes. Open lid and put cheese slices.

5. Cook for 3 minutes. Garnish with salad. Serve and enjoy!!!

Taco Soup

Preparation Time: 5 minutes

Cook Time: 10 minutes

Total Time: 15 minutes

Serve: 16

Calories: 200 kcal

Ingredients:

For Seasoning Blend:

- 1 Tbsp. cumin ground
- 2 Tsp. smoked paprika
- 2 Tsp. salt
- 1 Tsp. chipotle

For Taco Soup:

- 15 Oz. black beans canned, drained
- 4 Carrots
- 1 Onion Vidalia, diced
- 1 Lb. ground beef
- 9 Oz. chorizo pork
- 4 Cups of beef stock
- 14.5 Oz. fire roasted tomatoes
- 2 Cups of corn frozen, drained
- 1 Bunch of cilantro, chopped
- 1 Bell pepper, sliced
- 1 Jalapeno pepper, sliced

Cooking Instructions:

1. Place onion, ground beef and chorizo into the inner pot of the Ninja Foodi. Set the Ninja Foodi to sauté function.

2. Add the seasoning blend. Stir and sauté for about 10 minutes. Deglaze the pot with beef stock and stir around to make sure nothing is stuck to the bottom.

3. Put the tomatoes, black beans, carrots, corn, bell peppers, stems from the bunch of cilantro, and half of the jalapeno pepper.

4. Put the pressure lid on and be sure the valve is in seal position. Select high pressure and set to cook for 5 minutes.

5. When the cooking cycle is up, do quick pressure release for 5 minutes. Scoop the soup into serving plates.

6. Serve and enjoy!!!

Alphabet Vegetable Soup

Preparation Time: 10 minutes

Cook Time: 3 hours

Total Time: 3 hours 10 minutes

Serve: 4

Calories: 378 kcal

Ingredients:

- 1 Can of diced tomatoes
- 8 Cups of beef broth
- 3 Carrots, chopped
- 2 Celery, chopped
- 2 Potatoes, chopped
- 1 Large onion, chopped
- ½ Green pepper, chopped
- 1 Can of corn, drained
- 1 Can of green beans, drained
- 1 Can of peas, drained
- 1 Can of kidney beans, drained

Cooking Instructions:

1. In a small mixing bowl, merge together all ingredients except the pasta. Set the Ninja Foodi to slow cook high for 3 hours.

2. When the cooking cycle is over, set the Ninja Foodi to stovetop high. Put pasta and cook to your desired consistency.

3. Serve and enjoy!!!

Anasazi Bean and Ham Hock Soup

Preparation Time: 10 minutes

Cook Time: 20 minutes

Total Time: 30 minutes

Serve: 4

Calories: 332 kcal

Ingredients:

- 4 Stalk celery sliced
- 6 Cups of water
- 1 Lb. dry Anasazi bean
- 4 Meaty ham hocks
- 1 Onion, rough chopped
- ½ Lb. carrots, chopped

Cooking Instructions:

1. Set the Ninja Foodi to sauté function. Put the ham hocks and vegetables and sauté to your desired consistency.

2. Put beans and 6 cups of water. Put the pressure lid on and be sure the valve is in seal position. Select high pressure and set to cook for 20 minutes.

3. When the cooking cycle is up, do quick pressure release for 5 minutes. Open the lid and add 1 Tbsp. of dried thyme leaves. Scoop onto a serving plate.

4. Serve and enjoy!!!

Autumn Soup

Preparation Time: 10 minutes

Cook Time: 25 minutes

Total Time: 35 minutes

Serve: 4

Calories: 420 kcal

Ingredients:

- 1 ⅓ Lbs. lean ground beef
- 2 Quarts tomatoes, pureed with hand blender, about 7 cups
- 2 Cups of onions, diced
- 3 Cups of carrots, diced
- 3 Cups of celery, dices
- 6 Cups of potatoes, diced
- 4 Bay leaves
- Italian seasoning
- 2 Tbsp. beef base
- Pepper

Cooking Instructions:

1. Set the Ninja Foodi to sauté function. Put the beef and sauté to your desired consistency. Put tomatoes, onions, carrots, celery, potatoes, and bay leaves.

2. Add the Italian seasoning, beef base and pepper. Put the pressure lid on and be sure the valve is in seal position.

3. Select high pressure and set to cook for 25 minutes. When the cooking cycle is up, do quick pressure release for 5 minutes. Open the lid and remove the bay leaves. Serve and enjoy!!!

Easy Clam Chowder

Preparation Time: 10 minutes

Cook Time: 25 minutes

Total Time: 35 minutes

Serve: 4

Calories: 420 kcal

Ingredients:

- 5 Slices of bacon, sliced
- ¾ Cup of onions, chopped
- 2 Cans of chopped clams
- 4 Cups of water
- 1 Package of Idahoan Creamy Potato Soup Mix

Cooking Instructions:

1. Set the Ninja Foodi to sauté function. Put the bacon and onions and sauté to your desired consistency.

2. Put both cans of clams, and 4 cups of water. Put the pressure lid on and be sure the valve is in seal position. Select high pressure and set to cook for 25 minutes.

3. When the cooking cycle is up, do quick pressure release for 5 minutes. Open the lid and scoop the soup onto a serving plate.

4. Serve and enjoy!!!

Bacon Cheeseburger Soup

Preparation Time: 10 minutes

Cook Time: 8 minutes

Total Time: 18 minutes

Serve: 4

Calories: 328 kcal

Ingredients:

- 16 Oz. shredded cheddar cheese
- Salt
- 12 Oz. thick cut bacon
- 1 Lb. lean ground beef. Chopped
- ¼ Cup of flour
- 1 Tbsp. Montreal Steak Seasoning
- 2 Tsp. paprika
- 4 Cups of half and half
- 12 Oz. beer

Cooking Instructions:

1. Set the Ninja Foodi to sauté function. Put the bacon and beef and sauté to your desired consistency.

2. Drain the meat mixture; add seasoning, beer, flour, half and half. Stir thoroughly. Put the pressure lid on and be sure the valve is in seal position.

3. Select high pressure and set to cook for 8 minutes. When the cooking cycle is up, do quick pressure release for 5 minutes.

4. Open the lid and add cheese. Set the Ninja Foodi to warm function and allow the cheese to melt. Scoop the soup onto a serving plate.

5. Serve and enjoy!!!

Bear Creek Cheddar Potato Soup Mix

Preparation Time: 10 minutes

Cook Time: 2 hours

Total Time: 2 hours 10 minutes

Serve: 2

Calories: 400 kcal

Ingredients:

- Pepper
- 1 each Cheddar and Mexican Fiesta Cheese packages (8 Oz. each)
- 2 Cups of milk
- 2 Cups of water
- Potatoes, cubed
- Nature's Seasoning
- Salt

Cooking Instructions:

1. Microwave your potatoes for about 5 minutes. Set Ninja Foodi to Slow Cook High to cook for 2 hours.

2. Dump all the ingredients into the Ninja Foodi except the cheese. Lock the lid and cook for 2 hours. Add cheese after one hour of the cooking time.

3. Serve and enjoy!!!

Beef and Barley Soup

Preparation Time: 10 minutes

Cook Time: 5

Total Time: 15 minutes

Serve: 2

Calories: 386 kcal

Ingredients:

- 8 Oz. can of mushrooms
- 64 Oz. beef broth
- 2 Lbs. ground beef
- 2 Large carrots, chopped
- 7 Stalks celery, chopped
- 4 Bay leaves
- 2 Envelopes of Lipton beefy onion soup mix
- 11 Oz. box Quaker Quick Barley
- 1 Large sweet onion, chopped

Cooking Instructions:

1. Set the Ninja Foodi to sauté function. Put the beef, Onions, carrots and celery. Sauté to your desired consistency.

2. Dump in mushrooms, soup mix, broth, barley and bay leaves into the Ninja Foodi. Put the pressure lid on and be sure the valve is in seal position.

3. Select high pressure and set to cook for 5 minutes. When the cooking cycle is up, do quick pressure release for 10 minutes. Open the lid and remove the bay leaves.

4. Serve and enjoy!!!

NINJA FOODI RICE & PASTA RECIPES

Spaghetti Bolognese Sauce

Preparation Time: 10 minutes

Cook Time: 8 hours

Total Time: 8 hours 10 minutes

Serve: 8

Calories: 386 kcal

Ingredients:

- 1 Tsp. black pepper
- ½ Tsp. crushed red pepper flakes
- 2 Tbsp. olive oil
- 1 Lb. ground beef
- 1 Lb. ground Italian sausage
- 1 Onion minced
- 2 Carrots, chopped
- 8 Cloves of garlic minced
- 14 Oz. cans crushed tomatoes
- 24 Oz. jar of your favorite marinara sauce
- 1 Cup of water
- 3 Bay leaves
- 3 Tsp. better than chicken bouillon
- 3 Tsp. dried basil
- 2 Tsp. balsamic vinegar
- 2 Tsp. dried oregano
- 2 Tsp. sugar
- 2 Tsp. kosher salt
- 2 Tsp. dried parsley

- ½ Tsp. dried thyme

Cooking Instructions:

1. Set the Ninja Foodi to sauté function. Put the beef, Onions, carrots and garlic. Sauté for about 6-7 minutes or to your desired consistency.

2. Use a colander to drain the excess grease out. Put the meat mixture into the inner pot of the Ninja Foodi. Dump in the remaining ingredients and stir properly.

3. Put the pressure lid on and be sure the valve is in seal position. Select high pressure and set to cook for 5 minutes.

4. When the cooking cycle is up, do quick pressure release for 10 minutes. Open the lid and scoop the soup onto a serving plate.

5. Serve and enjoy!!!

Spanish Rice

Preparation Time: 5 minutes

Cook Time: 12 minutes

Total Time: 17 minutes

Serve: 4

Calories: 255 kcal

Ingredients:

- 1 Cups of uncooked long grain rice
- ½ Tsp. salt
- 1 Lb. ground beef
- 1 Small onion chopped
- 1 Chopped green pepper
- 1 Garlic clove, minced
- 1 Tbsp. chili powder
- 2 Cups of vegetable juice

Cooking Instructions:

1. Set the Ninja Foodi to sauté function. Put the ground beef. Sauté for about 5 minutes or to your desired consistency.

2. Dump in onion, green pepper, garlic and Chili powder. Sauté to your desired consistency. Dump in the rest of the ingredients and stir thoroughly.

3. Put the pressure lid on and be sure the valve is in seal position. Select high pressure and set to cook for 12 minutes.

4. When the cooking cycle is up, do quick pressure release for 10 minutes. Open the lid and scoop the soup onto a serving plate. Serve and enjoy!!!

Quick Chicken and Rice

Preparation Time: 10 minutes

Cook Time: 33 minutes

Total Time: 43 minutes

Serve: 4

Calories: 419 kcal

Ingredients:

- ⅛ Tsp. cayenne pepper
- 1 Bag (16 Oz.) frozen peas and carrots
- 2 Tbsp. extra-virgin olive oil
- 1 Lb. mushrooms, cleaned, sliced
- 2 Cups of long grain brown rice
- ½ Cups of white wine
- 2 Cups of chicken stock
- 2 Lbs. boneless, skinless chicken thighs
- 1 Tbsp. kosher salt
- 2 Tsp. smoked paprika
- 2 Tsp. granulated garlic
- 2 Tsp. onion powder
- 3 Sprigs of fresh thyme
- ½ Tsp. ground white pepper

Cooking Instructions:

1. Set the Ninja Foodi to sauté function. Put the oil and mushroom. Sauté for about 5 minutes or to your desired consistency.

2. Exception of frozen peas and carrots, dump in the rest of the ingredients and stir thoroughly.

3. Put the pressure lid on and be sure the valve is in seal position. Select high pressure and set to cook for 22 minutes.

4. When the cooking cycle is up, do quick pressure release for 10 minutes. Open the lid and put the frozen peas and carrots and allow to heat for 5 minutes.

5. Serve and enjoy!!!

Mac and Cheese with Bacon

Preparation Time: 5 minutes

Cook Time: 15 minutes

Total Time: 20 minutes

Serve: 14

Calories: 276 kcal

Ingredients:

- 1 Cup of Unsweetened Almond Milk
- 6 Oz. Freshly Shredded Cheddar Cheese, divided
- 1 Oz. Freshly Shredded Parmesan
- 8 Oz. Banza Pasta Elbows
- 2 Bacon, cut into strips
- 4 Cloves of (15g) Garlic, minced
- 2 Cups of (480mL) Chicken Broth

Optional Seasoning:

- 1 Tsp. Dry Mustard
- 1 Tsp. Parsley Flakes
- ½ Tsp. Black Pepper
- ¼ Tsp. Ground Nutmeg
- ¼ Tsp. Salt

Cooking Instructions:

1. Set the Ninja Foodi to sauté function. Put the bacon. Sauté for about 5 minutes or to your desired consistency. Remove into a paper towel.

2. Dump in garlic and continue sautéing for about 30 seconds. Add the chicken broth and uncooked pasta. Give it a nice stir.

3. Put the pressure lid on and be sure the valve is in seal position. Select high pressure and set to cook for 3 minutes.

4. When the cooking cycle is up, do quick pressure release for 10 minutes. Open the lid and add milk. Stir in Shredded cheese.

5. When you see that everything is melted, add the cooked bacon and the dry spices. Add cheddar and broil for 3 minutes.

6. Serve and enjoy!!!

Taco Pasta Bake

Preparation Time: 5 minutes

Cook Time: 30 minutes

Total Time: 35 minutes

Serve: 9

Calories: 276 kcal

Ingredients:

- 1 Box (8oz.) Banza Pasta Shells
- 1¼ Cup of low Fat Mexican Cheese Blend
- 1 Lb. 96 Ground Beef
- 1 Packet of Taco Seasoning
- 1 Packet of Ranch Dip Mix
- 10 Oz. Diced tomatoes with green chilies
- 15 Oz can of Pinto Beans, undrained

Cooking Instructions:

1. Begin by cooking the pasta according to manufacturer's instructions. Set the Ninja Foodi to sauté function.

2. Put the ground beef. Sauté to your desired consistency. Dump in taco, ranch seasoning, tomatoes, and Pinto beans into the Ninja Foodi.

3. Give it a thorough mix. Sauté for another 5 minutes. Drain the water and add pasta. Mix well and turn into the inner pot of the Ninja Foodi.

4. Top with Shredded cheese on the top. Put the pressure lid on and be sure the valve is in seal position. Select high pressure and set to cook for 20 minutes.

5. When the cooking cycle is up, do quick pressure release for 10 minutes. Open the lid, and flip the pasta onto a serving plate.

6. Serve and enjoy!!!

Cajun Sausage Pasta Bake

Preparation Time: 20 minutes

Cook Time: 15 minutes

Total Time: 35 minutes

Serve: 8

Calories: 290 kcal

Ingredients:

- 1 Red Bell Pepper, chopped
- 4 Turkey Sausages, sliced
- 8 Oz. (dry) Banza Penne
- 1 Cup of (244g) Light Alfredo Sauce
- ½ Cup of (120g) Marinara
- 2 Tsp. Cajun Seasoning
- ½ Cup of (56g) Shredded Cheddar
- 1 Zucchini, chopped

Cooking Instructions:

1. Begin by cooking the pasta according to manufacturer's instructions. Set the Ninja Foodi to sauté function.

2. Put the zucchini, red bell pepper and sausages. Sauté for about 12 minutes or to your desired consistency.

3. In a small mixing bowl, merge together the Alfredo, marinara and Cajun seasoning. Pour the sauce into the sausage. Stir thoroughly.

4. Drain the pasta and add to the sauce. Place the mixture in the basket of the Ninja Foodi and top with cheese and fresh parsley.

5. Put the pressure lid on and be sure the valve is in seal position. Select high pressure and set to cook for 15 minutes.

6. When the cooking cycle is up, do quick pressure release for 10 minutes. Open the lid, and flip the pasta onto a serving plate.

7. Serve and enjoy!!!

Mexican Rice

Preparation Time: 5 minutes

Cook Time: 23 minutes

Total Time: 28 minutes

Serve: 6

Calories: 178 kcal

Ingredients:

- 1½ Tsp. cumin
- 1½ Tsp. smoked paprika
- 2 Tbsp. vegetable oil
- 1 Cup of basmati rice
- ½ Green pepper diced
- 1 Onion about 1 cup
- 1 Carrot diced
- ½ Red bell pepper diced
- 1 Jalapeno pepper diced
- 2 Tbsp. tomato paste
- 2 Cups of water
- 1½ Tsp. sea salt

Cooking Instructions:

1. Set the Ninja Foodi to sauté function. Put the oil, rice, carrots and celery. Sauté to your desired consistency.

2. Add the vegetables and seasoning blend. Give it a good stir and then sauté for 5 minutes. Put the tomato paste and water.

3. Put the pressure lid on and be sure the valve is in seal position. Select high pressure and set to cook for 8 minutes.

4. When the cooking cycle is up, do quick pressure release for 10 minutes. Open the lid, and turn the rice onto a serving plate.

5. Serve and enjoy!!!

Pepperoni Pasta Salad

Preparation Time: 2 minutes

Cook Time: 3 minutes

Total Time: 5 minutes

Serve: 8

Calories: 579 kcal

Ingredients:

- Pepper
- 4 Cups of water
- 16 Oz. macaroni, dried-not cooked
- 1 Cup of mayonnaise
- ½ Cup of black olives, sliced and drained
- ½ Cup of pepperoni, quartered
- ¾ Cup of mozzarella cheese (cut into pieces)
- ½ Cup of Italian dressing
- ½ Cup of carrots, shredded
- ¾ Cup of Colby jack cheese, diced
- ¼ Cup of parmesan cheese, grated
- Salt

Cooking Instructions:

1. Begin by pouring the water into the Ninja Foodi liner. Add 1 Lb. of dried pasta and small salt. Do not stir rather push the pasta down to be fully cover by the water.

2. Put the pressure lid on and be sure the valve is in seal position. Select high pressure and set to cook for 3 minutes.

3. When the cooking cycle is up, do quick pressure release for 10 minutes. Open the lid, rinse the pasta and allow it to cool.

4. Mix together cooked macaroni and other ingredients in a large mixing bowl and put in the refrigerator.

5. Serve and enjoy!!!

Queso Mac and Cheese with Spicy Ground Beef

Preparation Time: 10 minutes

Cook Time: 20 minutes

Total Time: 30 minutes

Serve: 6

Calories: 353 kcal

Ingredients:

- 8 Oz. Banza Pasta Elbows
- 12 Oz. jar Queso Dip
- 1 Lb. Lean Ground Beef
- 1 Tbsp. (16g) Olive Oil
- 2 Tsp. Ground Chipotle Chili Powder
- 1 Tsp. Garlic Powder
- 1 Tsp. Onion Powder
- 1 Tsp. White Pepper
- 1 Tsp. Kosher Salt
- ¼ Cup of (60g) Chipotle Cholula Hot Sauce

Cooking Instructions:

1. Cook the pasta according to the instructions on the package. Set the Ninja Foodi to sauté function. Put the oil and ground beef. Sauté to your desired consistency.

2. In a small mixing bowl, merge together the spices and add this mixture to the ground beef. Give it a nice stir and continue sautéing to your desired consistency.

3. Add the chipotle Cholula and queso. Stir well and add the cooked pasta. Add cheese on the top.

4. Put the pressure lid on and be sure the valve is in seal position. Select high pressure and set to cook for 5 minutes.

5. When the cooking cycle is up, do quick pressure release for 10 minutes. Open the lid and flip onto a serving plate.

6. Serve and enjoy!!!

Healthy Pasta Salad

Preparation Time: 10 minutes

Cook Time: 10 minutes

Total Time: 20 minutes

Serve: 20

Calories: 412 kcal

Ingredients:

- 2 Tsp. Smoked Paprika
- 2 Tbsp. Chopped Fresh Parsley
- 16 Oz. (dry) Banza Rotini
- 1 Cup of (227g) Fat Free Greek Yogurt
- ½ Cup of (120g) Light Mayo
- ¼ Cup of (60g) Stone Ground Mustard
- 4 Oz. jar Diced Pimentos
- ¼ Cup of (60g) Dill Relish
- 1 Medium Red Onion, diced
- 1 Medium Green Bell Pepper, diced
- 2 Tsp. Black Pepper

Cooking Instructions:

1. Cook the pasta according to the instructions on the package. Dice the onion and bell pepper.

2. Combine the remaining ingredients in a small mixing bowl and add the onion and pepper. Give it a nice mix.

3. Place the Mixture in the Ninja Foodi, Put the pressure lid on and be sure the valve is in seal position. Select high pressure and set to cook for 2 minutes.

4. When the cooking cycle is up, do quick pressure release for 5 minutes. Open the lid and flip onto a serving plate and allow it to cool off.

5. Serve and enjoy!!!

NINJA FOODI BEANS & GRAIN RECIPES

Corn on the Cob

Preparation Time: 10 minutes

Cook Time: 2 minutes

Total Time: 12 minutes

Serve: 4

Calories: 1 kcal

Ingredients:

- 4 Ears corn
- 1 Cup of water
- Salt

Cooking Instructions:

1. Begin by pouring 1 cup water into Ninja Foodi. Place the corn on the Ninja Foodi steamer basket.

2. Put the pressure lid on and be sure the valve is in seal position. Select high pressure and set to cook for 2 minutes.

3. When the cooking cycle is up, do quick pressure release for 5 minutes. Open the lid, add salt and transfer onto a serving plate.

4. Serve and enjoy!!!

Green Beans

Preparation Time: 10 minutes

Cook Time: 1 minute

Total Time: 11 minutes

Serve: 8

Calories: 109 kcal

Ingredients:

- Pinch of pepper
- ½ Cup of vegetable broth
- 2 Lbs. Fresh whole green beans, stems removed
- 6 Strips of bacon, cut into small pieces
- ¼ Cup of almonds, sliced
- ¼ Cup of cranberries, dried
- 1 Tsp. garlic, minced
- Pinch of salt

Cooking Instructions:

1. Set the Ninja Foodi to sauté function. Put the bacon. Sauté to your desired consistency. Switch off the sauté function, add garlic and cranberries. Stir well.

2. Add sliced almonds, salt, pepper, fresh green beans and the broth. Give it a nice mix. Put the pressure lid on and be sure the valve is in seal position.

3. Select high pressure and set to cook for 1 minute. When the cooking cycle is up, do quick pressure release for 5 minutes.

4. Open the lid, stir and transfer onto a serving plate. Serve and enjoy!!!

Barbequed Baked Beans

Preparation Time: 10 minutes

Cook Time: 1 hour

Total Time: 1 hour 10 minutes

Serve: 4

Calories: 287 kcal

Ingredients:

- 2 Tbsp. bottled hot sauce
- 8 Dashes of liquid smoke
- 16 Oz. dried kidney beans, soaked overnight
- 6 Cups of water
- 1 Medium onion, chopped
- 1½ Cups of ketchup
- ½ Cup of molasses
- ½ Cup of brown sugar
- 2 Tbsp. Dijon mustard

Cooking Instructions:

1. Drain the beans, rinse, put enough water. Put it in the inner pot of the Ninja Foodi. Bring to a boil on stovetop high and allow it to simmer for an hour.

2. Drain well in colander. Rinse out Ninja and place beans back in crock. Mix together remaining ingredients and mix into beans.

3. Put the pressure lid on and be sure the valve is in seal position. Select high pressure and set to cook for 1 hour.

4. When the cooking cycle is up, do quick pressure release for 5 minutes. Open the lid. Flip onto a serving plate.

5. Serve and enjoy!!!

Black Bean and Beef Taco Soup

Preparation Time: 10 minutes

Cook Time: 1 hour

Total Time: 1 hour 10 minutes

Serve: 4

Calories: 412 kcal

Ingredients:

- 2 Tbsp. beef bouillon powder
- 2 Cups of water
- 1 Lb. of ground beef
- 1 Diced onion
- 3 Cloves of garlic, chopped
- 1 Pint jar of home canned black beans, rinsed
- 1 Pint jar of corn
- 1½ Cups of pre-cooked rice
- 2 Tbsp. taco seasoning
- 1 Quart of home canned beef broth
- 1 Quart of home canned tomato broth

Cooking Instructions:

1. Set the Ninja Foodi to stovetop high. Put the meat and onions and sauté to your desired consistency.

2. Dump in the taco seasoning, corn, black beans, pre-cooked rice, broths, water and beef bouillon powder. Give it a nice mix.

3. Set the Ninja Foodi to Stove Top Medium function to cook for about 1 hour. Put the pressure lid on and be sure the valve is in seal position.

4. Select high pressure and set to cook for 1 hour. When the cooking cycle is up, do quick pressure release for 5 minutes. Open the lid. Flip onto a serving plate.

5. Serve and enjoy!!!

Black Bean Chili

Preparation Time: 10 minutes

Cook Time: 8 hours

Total Time: 8 hours 10 minutes

Serve: 4

Calories: 286 kcal

Ingredients:

- ½ Onion, chopped
- 28 Oz. can diced tomatoes
- 1 ½ Lbs. Turkey
- 16 Oz. dry black beans
- 3 Cups of water
- 2 Tbsp. chili powder
- 1 Tsp. cinnamon
- ½ Tsp. ground cloves
- 2 Tsp. sugar
- 1 Tsp. garlic powder

Cooking Instructions:

1. Set the Ninja Foodi to stovetop high. Put the meat and sauté to your desired consistency. Put the remaining ingredients.

2. Lock the Pressure lid, set the valve to sealing position and set to slow cook for 8 hours. When the cooking cycle is up, do quick pressure release for 5 minutes.

3. Open the lid. Flip onto a serving plate. Serve and enjoy!!!

Black-Eyed Peas Chili

Preparation Time: 10 minutes

Cook Time: 8 hours

Total Time: 8 hours 10 minutes

Serve: 4

Calories: 286 kcal

Ingredients:

- 1 (10 oz.) Can of tomatoes with green chilies, undrained
- 2 Tbsp. chili powder
- 1 Lb. bulk pork sausage
- 1 Medium onion, chopped
- ½ Cup of celery, chopped
- 4 (15 Oz.) Cans of black-eyed peas, undrained
- 1 (14 Oz.) Can of diced tomatoes, undrained

Cooking Instructions:

1. Set the Ninja Foodi to stovetop high. Put the sausage, celery and onions. Sauté to your desired consistency.

2. Put the black-eyed peas, tomatoes, rotel, and chili powder. Lock the Pressure lid, set the valve to sealing position and set to slow cook for 30 minutes.

3. When the cooking cycle is up, do quick pressure release for 5 minutes. Open the lid. Flip onto a serving plate.

4. Serve and enjoy!!!

Baked Beans

Preparation Time: 10 minutes

Cook Time: 8 hours

Total Time: 8 hours 10 minutes

Serve: 4

Calories: 286 kcal

Ingredients:

- 1 Tsp. salt
- 1 Tsp. black pepper
- ¾ Lb. thick-cut bacon, diced
- 1 Large onion, diced
- 1 Lb. dried pinto beans
- 5 Cups of water
- ¾ Cup of unsulfured molasses
- ½ Cup of ketchup
- ¼ Cup of yellow mustard

Cooking Instructions:

1. Set the Ninja Foodi to stovetop high. Put the bacon, and onions. Sauté to your desired consistency. Put the beans and water into the Ninja Foodi.

2. Lock the Pressure lid, set the valve to sealing position and set to slow cook for 3 hours. When the cooking cycle is up, do quick pressure release for 5 minutes.

3. Prepare the sauce by mixing the molasses, ketchup, and mustard. Add salt, and pepper in a small bowl. Set aside for 3 hours.

4. Put the sauce into the Ninja Foodi and stir properly. Cover and let the beans cook an additional hour.

5. Serve and enjoy!?

Anasazi Bean and Ham Hock Soup

Preparation Time: 10 minutes

Cook Time: 12 hours

Total Time: 12 hours 10 minutes

Serve: 4

Calories: 385 kcal

Ingredients:

- 1 Lb. dry Anasazi bean
- 4 Meaty ham hocks
- 1 Onion, chopped
- ½ Lb. carrots, chopped
- 4 Stalk celery, sliced
- 6 Cups of water

Cooking Instructions:

1. Set the Ninja Foodi to stovetop high. Put the ham and vegetables. Sauté to your desired consistency. Put beans and 6 Cups of water.

2. Lock the Pressure lid, set the valve to sealing position and set to slow cook for 12 hours. When the cooking cycle is up, do quick pressure release for 10 minutes.

3. Open the lid, transfer the beans onto a serving plate and top with 1 Tbsp. of dried thyme leaves.

4. Serve and enjoy!!!

NINJA FOODI VEGETABLE RECIPES

Brussels Sprouts

Preparation Time: 5 minutes

Cook Time: 10 minutes

Total Time: 15 minutes

Serve: 1

Calories: 178 kcal

Ingredients:

- 1 Lb. Brussels Sprouts, Halved
- ½ Tsp. Garlic Salt
- Olive Oil Cooking Spray

Cooking Instructions:

1. Put the Brussels sprouts into the inner pot of the Ninja Foodi. Add salt and olive oil. Put the pressure lid on and be sure the valve is in seal position.

2. Select high pressure and set to cook for 10 minutes. When the cooking cycle is up, do quick pressure release for 10 minutes. Open the lid and flip onto serving plates.

3. Serve and enjoy!!!

Toasted Israeli Couscous with Vegetables

Preparation Time: 30 minutes

Cook Time: 30 minutes

Total Time: 60 minutes

Serve: 4

Calories: 289 kcal

Ingredients:

- Freshly ground black pepper
- Lemon-balsamic vinaigrette
- 225g Israeli couscous
- Salt
- 12 Spears asparagus, grilled and cut into pieces
- 1 Courgette, halved, grilled and cut into pieces
- 1 Yellow squash, halved, grilled and cut into pieces
- 2 Large red peppers, grilled, peeled and diced into bite-size pieces
- 40g Kalamata olives, pitted and chopped
- 2 Tbsp. chopped fresh basil leaves
- 1 Cup of hot water

For the lemon-balsamic vinaigrette:

- Salt and freshly ground black pepper
- 190ml Extra-virgin olive oil
- 1 Small shallot, minced
- 3 Tbsp. fresh lemon juice
- 1 Tsp. lemon zest
- 3 Tbsp. aged balsamic vinegar
- 1 Tbsp. wine vinegar

Cooking Instructions:

1. Set the Ninja Foodi to sauté mode. Dump in couscous and the vegetables. Sauté to your consistency. Add water and salt.

2. Sauté to your desired consistency. Drain well and place in a large bowl. Put the olives, basil, vinaigrette, salt and pepper.

3. Give it a nice mix. Place it on the Ninja Foodi and cook for 3 minutes.

4. Serve and enjoy!!!

Charred Vegetable and Couscous Salad

Preparation Time: 5 minutes

Cook Time: 20 minutes

Total Time: 25 minutes

Serve: 6

Calories: 335 kcal

Ingredients:

- 300g Couscous
- 1 Garlic clove
- 6 ¾ Tbsp. extra-virgin olive oil
- A Sprig of fresh thyme
- ½ Chicken stock cube
- Salt
- 8 Asparagus spears, peeled, cut in half
- ½ Bunch spring onions, chopped
- 1 Aubergine, cut into 2cm cubes
- 1 Courgette, cut into 2cm cubes
- 1 Red pepper, de-seeded, cut into 2cm cubes
- 75ml Red wine vinegar
- A handful of rocket leaves
- ½ Bunch fresh basil, shredded
- 1 Cup of hot water

Cooking Instructions:

1. Put the couscous in a small mixing bowl, put the hot water in the inner pot of the Ninja Foodi.

2. Add 3 ½ of olive oil, garlic, salt, thyme and the half stock cube. Season with salt. Add the couscous. Stir properly.

3. Put the pressure lid on and be sure the valve is in seal position. Select high pressure and set to cook for 3 minutes.

4. When the cooking cycle is up, do quick pressure release for 10 minutes. Open the lid, add the rocket and basil.

5. Serve and enjoy!!!

Buffalo Cauliflower

Preparation Time: 5 minutes

Cook Time: 15 minutes

Total Time: 20 minutes

Serve: 6

Calories: 335 kcal

Ingredients:

- ½ Tsp. Pepper
- 4 Cups Cauliflower Florets
- 4 Tbsp. Butter, Melted
- ½ Cup of Buffalo Sauce
- 1 Cup of Gluten-Free or Regular Bread Crumbs
- 1 Tbsp. Garlic Powder
- 1 Tsp. Salt

Cooking Instructions:

1. Merge together the butter, buffalo sauce and cauliflower in a small mixing bowl. In another bowl, merge together bread crumbs, garlic powder, salt, and pepper.

2. Coat each cauliflower with this mixture and arrange them in the inner pot of the Ninja Foodi. Put the pressure lid on and be sure the valve is in seal position.

3. Select high pressure and set to cook for 15 minutes. When the cooking cycle is up, do quick pressure release for 10 minutes. Open the lid, flip onto serving plates.

4. Serve and enjoy!!!

Saffron, Courgette and Herb Couscous

Preparation Time: 10 minutes

Cook Time: 20 minutes

Total Time: 30 minutes

Serve: 6

Calories: 411 kcal

Ingredients:

- 350ml chicken stock
- 1 Tsp. salt
- ½ Tsp. freshly ground black pepper
- ¼ Tsp. ground cumin
- ½ Tsp. saffron threads
- 2 Tbsp. olive oil
- 30g Unsalted butter, melted
- 2 Courgettes, large dice
- 285g Couscous
- 20g Basil leaves, chopped
- 20g Parsley leaves, chopped

Cooking Instructions:

1. Set the Ninja Foodi to sauté mode. Dump in salt, pepper, cumin, and saffron threads. Sauté to your desired consistency.

2. Add olive oil, melted butter, and courgette and continue sautéing to your desired consistency. Put the Caucasus, Courgette and chicken stock into a small mixing bowl.

3. Transfer the mixture into the Ninja Foodi. Put the pressure lid on and be sure the valve is in seal position. Select high pressure and set to cook for 20 minutes.

4. When the cooking cycle is up, do quick pressure release for 10 minutes. Open the lid, add basil and parsley. Flip onto serving plates.

5. Serve and enjoy!!!

Seasoned Asparagus

Preparation Time: 2 minutes

Cook Time: 10 minutes

Total Time: 12 minutes

Serve: 4

Calories: 290 kcal

Ingredients:

- 1 Bunch Asparagus, stem trimmed
- Garlic Salt

Cooking Instructions:

1. Put the Asparagus and garlic salt in the inner pot of the Ninja Foodi. Put the pressure lid on and be sure the valve is in seal position.

2. Select high pressure and set to cook for 10 minutes. When the cooking cycle is up, do quick pressure release for 10 minutes.

3. Serve and enjoy!!!

Steak and Vegetable Bowls

Preparation Time: 5 minutes

Cook Time: 15 minutes

Total Time: 20 minutes

Serve: 6

Calories: 311 kcal

Ingredients:

- Olive oil
- 2 KC Strip Steaks, cut into chunks
- 1 Cup of Red Bell Pepper, Diced
- 1 Cup of Green Bell Pepper, Diced
- 1 Cup of Yellow Squash, Diced
- 1 Cup of Mushroom, Sliced
- ¼ Cup of White Onion, Diced
- ½ Tbsp. Steak Seasoning

Cooking Instructions:

1. Spray the Ninja Foodi cooking basket with olive oil and arrange the Steaks and vegetables on the basket.

2. Add seasoning and spray with olive oil spray. Put the pressure lid on and be sure the valve is in seal position.

3. Select high pressure and set to cook for 15 minutes. When the cooking cycle is up, do quick pressure release for 10 minutes.

4. Serve and enjoy!!!

Vidalia Onions

Preparation Time: 15 minutes

Cook Time: 25 minutes

Total Time: 40 minutes

Serve: 2

Calories: 498 kcal

Ingredients:

- 2 Ice Cubes
- 2 Sheets of Foil
- 2 Vidalia Onions
- 2 Beef Bouillon Cubes
- 2 Tbsp. Butter

Cooking Instructions:

1. Peel the onion and calve a hole on the center of the onion. Lay the onion on a sheet of Foil. Insert the beef bouillon cube and butter on the onion hole.

2. Push it down to fit well. Add the ice cube on top of the hole and wrap the onion up in the foil. Do this for the other Onion.

3. Lay them on the basket of the Ninja Foodi. Put the pressure lid on and be sure the valve is in seal position.

4. Select high pressure and set to cook for 20 minutes. When the cooking cycle is up, do quick pressure release for 10 minutes. Flip on to serving plate.

5. Serve and enjoy!!!

Roasted Carrots

Preparation Time: 5 minutes

Cook Time: 15 minutes

Total Time: 20 minutes

Serve: 4

Calories: 224 kcal

Ingredients:

- 16 Oz. of carrots, chopped into chunks
- 1 Tsp. oil
- Salt
- Pepper

Cooking Instructions:

1. Put carrot and oil into the inner pot of the Ninja Foodi. Put the pressure lid on and be sure the valve is in seal position.

2. Select high pressure and set to cook for 15 minutes. When the cooking cycle is up, do quick pressure release for 10 minutes.

3. Open the lid, add salt and pepper. Flip on to serving plate.

4. Serve and enjoy!!!

NINJA FOODI APPETIZER RECIPES

Homemade Peanut Sauce

Preparation Time: 5 minutes

Cook Time: 5 minutes

Total Time: 10 minutes

Serve: 12

Calories: 76 kcal

Ingredients:

- ⅔ Cup of coconut milk
- 2 Tbsp. brown sugar
- 2 Tsp. soy sauce
- 2 Tbsp. water
- 1 Tbsp. red chili sauce
- 2 Cloves of garlic
- ⅓ Cup of peanut butter

Cooking Instructions:

1. Put the above ingredients in the order they are listed into Ninja Foodi Cold and Hot Blender. Select the heating function on medium and heat for 5 minutes.

2. Select the smoothie function. Immediately the smoothie function is completed, the sauce is fully cooked. Transfer to a serving plate.

3. Serve and enjoy!!!

Crab Rangoon

Preparation Time: 20 minutes

Cook Time: 10 minutes

Total Time: 30 minutes

Serve: 8

Calories: 76 kcal

Ingredients:

- 16 Wonton wrappers
- Olive oil
- 2 Oz. imitation crab meat
- 2 Oz. cream cheese room temp
- 1½ Tbsp. green onions chopped small
- ½ Tbsp. Worcestershire sauce

Cooking Instructions:

1. In a small mixing bowl, merge together the cream cheese, imitation crab meat, green onions, and Worcestershire sauce.

2. With the Air Fryer basket inside, preheat the Ninja Foodi on broil for 10 minutes. Fold up the crab Rangoon.

3. Put 8 Wonton wrappers in the cooling rack placing 1 Tsp. of filling in the center of each Wonton. Pour little water on the filling and fold into any shape.

4. Sprinkle oil on the basket and lay 8 crabs on it. Set the Ninja Foodi to AC function to cook for 5 minutes. Turnover, spray oil and cook for another 5 minutes.

5. Repeat this for all the crab. Serve and enjoy!!!

Meatballs

Preparation Time: 10 minutes

Cook Time: 10 minutes

Total Time: 20 minutes

Serve: 6

Calories: 232 kcal

Ingredients:

- 1 Lb. ground beef
- 1½ Tbsp. Worcestershire sauce
- ¾ Tsp. sea salt
- ¾ Tsp. black pepper
- ¾ Tsp. basil
- ¾ Tsp. onion powder
- ¾ Tsp. garlic powder
- 1 Large egg
- ⅓ Cup of bread crumbs

Cooking Instructions:

1. In a small mixing bowl, merge together the ground beef, seasonings, Worcestershire sauce, egg, and bread crumbs.

2. With the Air Fryer basket inside, preheat the Ninja Foodi on broil for 10 minutes. Give it a good mix.

3. Create meatballs using about 2 Tbsp. of mixture per meatball. Spritz the preheated Ninja Foodi basket with oil.

4. Place meatballs on the bottom of the basket. Put the pressure lid on and be sure the valve is in seal position. Select high pressure and set to cook for 10 minutes.

5. When the cooking cycle is up, do quick pressure release for 10 minutes. Open the lid and flip the meatballs on to a serving plate.

6. Serve and enjoy!!!

Oreos

Preparation Time: 5 minutes

Cook Time: 5 minutes

Total Time: 10 minutes

Serve: 1

Calories: 225 kcal

Ingredients:

- 1 Tube Crescent Rolls
- 8 Oreos

Cooking Instructions:

1. Use crescent rolls to wrap the Oreos and trim out unnecessary parts of the crescent.

2. Spray the Ninja Foodi basket with cooking spray of your choice. Arrange the peanut butter cups in the Ninja Foodi basket.

3. Put the pressure lid on and be sure the valve is in seal position. Select high pressure and set to cook for 5 minutes.

4. When the cooking cycle is up, do quick pressure release for 10 minutes. Open the lid and transfer on to a serving plate.

5. Serve and enjoy!!!

Football Deviled Eggs

Preparation Time: 10 minutes

Cook Time: 5 minutes

Total Time: 15 minutes

Serve: 1

Calories: 116 kcal

Ingredients:

- 12 Hard cooked eggs, peeled and cut lengthwise
- 4 Tbsp. mayonnaise
- 2 Tbsp. sweet pickle juice
- 4 Tsp. spicy brown mustard
- Salt
- Pepper

Cooking Instructions:

1. Add 1 cup of water into the inner pot of the Ninja Foodi. Arrange the eggs into the pot. Put the pressure lid on and be sure the valve is in seal position.

2. Select high pressure and set to cook for 5 minutes. When the cooking cycle is up, do quick pressure release for 10 minutes.

3. Open the lid and transfer the eggs into cool water and keep for sometimes. When it is cool enough to handle with your hands, peel the eggs and cut lengthwise.

4. With a food processor, mix the egg yolks, mayonnaise, pickle juice, mustard, salt and pepper until smooth. Put yolk mixture into each egg white.

5. Serve and enjoy!!!

Lasagna Dip

Preparation Time: 10 minutes

Cook Time: 8 minutes

Total Time: 18 minutes

Serve: 1

Calories: 69 kcal

Ingredients:

- 1 ½ Lb. ground beef
- 1 Jar (24 Oz.) spaghetti sauce
- 2 Cups of ricotta cheese
- 2 Cups of mozzarella, shredded

Cooking Instructions:

1. Set the Ninja Foodi to sauté mode. Dump in ground beef and spaghetti sauce and sauté to your desired preference.

2. Add large dollops of ricotta cheese on top of the beef mixture. Spread out evenly. Sprinkle shredded mozzarella cheese on the top.

3. Put the pressure lid on and be sure the valve is in seal position. Select high pressure and set to cook for 8 minutes.

4. When the cooking cycle is up, do quick pressure release for 10 minutes. Open the lid and transfer on to a serving plate.

5. Serve and enjoy!!!

Peanut Butter Cups

Preparation Time: 10 minutes

Cook Time: 6 minutes

Total Time: 16 minutes

Serve: 1

Calories: 109 kcal

Ingredients:

- 1 Tube Crescent Rolls
- 8 Peanut Butter Cups

Cooking Instructions:

1. Use crescent rolls to wrap the peanut butter cups and trim out unnecessary parts of the crescent.

2. Spray the Ninja Foodi basket with cooking spray of your choice. Arrange the peanut butter cups in the Ninja Foodi basket.

3. Put the pressure lid on and be sure the valve is in seal position. Select high pressure and set to cook for 6 minutes.

4. When the cooking cycle is up, do quick pressure release for 10 minutes. Open the lid and transfer on to a serving plate.

5. Serve and enjoy!!!

Roasted Garlic

Preparation Time: 5 minutes

Cook Time: 35 minutes

Total Time: 40 minutes

Serve: 5

Calories: 26 kcal

Ingredients:

- 5 Bulbs of garlic, stem trimmed out
- 1 Tbsp. olive oil

Cooking Instructions:

1. Lay the garlic bulb in an aluminum foil and sprinkle with oil. Place the foil in the inner pot of the Ninja Foodi.

2. Put the pressure lid on and be sure the valve is in seal position. Select high pressure and set to cook for 35 minutes.

3. When the cooking cycle is up, do quick pressure release for 10 minutes. Open the lid and transfer on to a serving plate.

4. Serve and enjoy!!!

Peppers

Preparation Time: 5 minutes

Cook Time: 12 minutes

Total Time: 17 minutes

Serve: 6

Calories: 40 kcal

Ingredients:

- ¼ Tsp. garlic salt
- 1 Tbsp. olive oil
- 3 Bell peppers, sliced, top and seed discarded
- ¼ Tsp. Old Bay
- ¼ Tsp. onion powder

Cooking Instructions:

1. Slice the pepper into strips. Dump them into a small mixing bowl and then add oil and the seasoning. Mix thoroughly.

2. Pour the mixture into the Ninja Foodi basket spreading out evenly. Put the pressure lid on and be sure the valve is in seal position.

3. Select high pressure and set to cook for 12 minutes. When the cooking cycle is up, do quick pressure release for 10 minutes.

4. Open the lid and transfer on to a serving plate.

5. Serve and enjoy!!!

Pineapple Sweet and Sour Sauce

Preparation Time: 6 minutes

Cook Time: 6 minutes

Total Time: 12 minutes

Serve: 8

Calories: 44 kcal

Ingredients:

- ¼ Cup of sugar
- ¼ Tsp. red pepper flakes
- 2 Tsp. corn starch
- 8 Oz. crushed pineapple with juice
- 2 Tbsp. rice vinegar

Cooking Instructions:

1. Merge together the cornstarch and 1 Tbsp. of juice from the pineapple. Give it a thorough mix.

2. Add the remaining pineapple with juice, cornstarch, sugar, rice vinegar, and red pepper flakes into the Ninja Foodi Cold and Hot Blender.

3. Put the pressure lid on and be sure the valve is in seal position. Select high pressure and set to cook for 6 minutes.

4. When the cooking cycle is up, do quick pressure release for 10 minutes. Open the lid and transfer on to a serving plate.

5. Serve and enjoy!!!

NINJA FOODI DESSERT RECIPES

Apple Fritter

Preparation Time: 10 minutes

Cook Time: 15 minutes

Total Time: 25 minutes

Serve: 1

Calories: 374 kcal

Ingredients:

- 1 Tbsp. (14g) Butter
- 3 Tbsp. (42g) Fat Free Greek Yogurt
- ½ Cup of (60g) All Purpose Flour
- 2 Tbsp. (24g) Brown Sugar
- 1 Tsp. Baking Powder
- ¼ Tsp. Kosher Salt
- ½ Tsp. Ground Cinnamon
- ⅛ Tsp. Ground Nutmeg
- ½ Pink Lady Apple, (40g) peeled and diced

For the Glaze:

- 2 Tbsp. (18g) Powdered Sugar
- ½ Tbsp. (7g) Water

Cooking Instructions:

1. Begin by combining the flour, brown sugar, baking powder, salt, cinnamon, and nutmeg in a large bowl. Cut the butter using pastry blender.

2. Carefully dump in the apple and Greek yogurt. Stir thoroughly. Pour the mixture on a tray or any flat surface and use your hands to form a ball of dough.

3. Press and flatten the dough into oval shape. Sprinkle the Ninja Foodi basket with oil and arrange the dough on the basket.

4. Put the pressure lid on and be sure the valve is in seal position. Select high pressure and set to cook for 15 minutes.

5. When the cooking cycle is up, do quick pressure release for 10 minutes. Open the lid and transfer on to a serving plate.

6. For the glaze, mix the powdered sugar and water together and pour on top of the fritter as it comes out of the Ninja Foodi.

7. Serve and enjoy!!!

Domino's Cinnamon Bread Twists

Preparation Time: 15 minutes

Cook Time: 15 minutes

Total Time: 30 minutes

Serve: 6

Calories: 221 kcal

Ingredients:

For the Bread Twists Dough:

- 1 Cup of (120g) All Purpose Flour
- 1 Tsp. Baking Powder
- ¼ Tsp. Kosher Salt
- ⅔ Cup of (150g) Fat Free Greek Yogurt

For Brushing on the Cooked Bread Twists:

- 2 Tbsp. (28g) Light Butter
- 2 Tbsp. (24g) Granulated Sugar
- 1 Tsp. Ground Cinnamon

Cooking Instructions:

1. In a small mixing bowl, merge together the flour, baking powder, salt and Greek yogurt. Give it a thorough mix with a fork.

2. Pour the mixture on a tray or any flat surface and use your hands to form a ball of dough. Divide it into 6 portions. Roll the dough and form thin strips.

3. Flatten and roll one end of each strip to form ribbon shape. Repeat this for all the dough and arrange them in the Ninja Foodi basket. Spray with oil.

4. Put the pressure lid on and be sure the valve is in seal position. Select high pressure and set to cook for 15 minutes.

5. When the cooking cycle is up, do quick pressure release for 10 minutes. Open the lid and check for doneness.

6. Microwave the light butter, granulated sugar, and cinnamon. Give it a thorough stir. Brush the mixture on top of the bread twists.

7. Serve and enjoy.

Pumpkin Pie Custard Cups

Preparation Time: 5 minutes

Cook Time: 7 minutes

Total Time: 12 minutes

Serve: 8

Calories: 211 kcal

Ingredients:

- ¾ Cup of half and half
- 1 Cup of heavy whipping cream
- 3 Large eggs
- ⅓ Cup of sugar
- ½ Cup of pumpkin puree
- 2 Tbsp. vanilla extract
- 2 Tsp. pumpkin pie spice

Cooking Instructions:

1. In a medium mixing bowl, merge together the eggs, sugar, canned pumpkin and pumpkin pie spice. Give it a nice stir.

2. Dump in vanilla extract, half & half and heavy whipping cream. Mix well and pour mixture into 8 canning jars. Add into the Ninja Foodi and put a cup of water.

3. Put the pressure lid on and be sure the valve is in seal position. Select high pressure and set to cook for 7 minutes.

4. When the cooking cycle is up, do quick pressure release for 10 minutes. Open the lid, remove the jars and allow it to cool. Top with pumpkin pie spice. Serve!!!

Brownies

Preparation Time: 5 minutes

Cook Time: 4 hours

Total Time: 4 hours 5 minutes

Serve: 16

Calories: 248 kcal

Ingredients:

- ⅓ Cup of cocoa powder unsweetened
- 1¼ Cup of flour all purpose
- ½ Cup of butter, salted
- 4 Oz. dark chocolate chips
- 4 Oz. milk chocolate chips
- 1 Cup of sugar
- 2 Tbsp. canola oil
- 1 Tbsp. vanilla extract
- 3 Large eggs slightly beaten

Cooking Instructions:

1. Set the Ninja Foodi to sauté mode. Dump in butter and chocolate chips. Stir and sauté to your preference. Add sugar and stir.

2. Beat the eggs and pour it into the batter. Put vanilla extract and give it a nice mix. Put the Unsweetened cocoa powder and flour. Stir thoroughly.

3. Put the pressure lid on and be sure the valve is in seal position. Select high pressure and set to slow cook for 4 hours.

4. When the cooking cycle is up, do quick pressure release for 10 minutes. Open the lid and flip the Brownie onto a serving plate.

5. Serve and enjoy!!!

Christmas Tree Brownies

Preparation Time: 5 minutes

Cook Time: 10 minutes

Total Time: 15 minutes

Serve: 3

Calories: 230 kcal

Ingredients:

- Brownies baked in a square pan
- Vanilla icing
- Green food coloring
- Piping bag
- Green decorating sugar
- Christmas light sprinkles
- Star sprinkles

Cooking Instructions:

1. Begin by cooking the Brownies according to package Instructions. When they are well cooked, remove and arrange them on a cutting board.

2. Slice the Brownies into half and then calf out triangle from each slice. Combine together the green food coloring and vanilla icing.

3. Put icing in a piping bag and fill the icing into each brownie. Top with green decorating sugar. Add a star sprinkle to the top of each tree.

4. Put the pressure lid on and be sure the valve is in seal position. Select high pressure and set to cook for a minute.

5. When the cooking cycle is up, do quick pressure release for 10 minutes. Open the lid and transfer Brownies to a serving container.

6. Serve and enjoy!!!

Baked Drunken Apples

Preparation Time: 10 minutes

Cook Time: 6 hours

Total Time: 6 hours 10 minutes

Serve: 3

Calories: 332 kcal

Ingredients:

- ½ Cup of whiskey
- Cinnamon
- 7 Medium sized apples cored halfway
- 1 Cup of ginger ale soda
- 1 Cup of brown sugar
- ⅓ Cup of raisins
- ⅓ Cup of walnuts, chopped

Cooking Instructions:

1. Begin by slicing the apple halfway to the center. Do not cut it out and arrange them in the inner pot of the Ninja Foodi.

2. In a small mixing bowl, merge together the brown sugar, raisins and walnuts. Scoop into the apples.

3. Mix whiskey and ginger together. Add the sugar mixture and mix well to combine. Pour it on top of the apples. Top with cinnamon.

4. Put the pressure lid on and be sure the valve is in seal position. Select high pressure and set to slow cook low for 6 hours.

5. When the cooking cycle is up, do quick pressure release for 10 minutes. Open the lid and transfer apple to a serving plate.

6. Serve and enjoy!!!

5 Ingredients Pumpkin Cake

Preparation Time: 10 minutes

Cook Time: 50 minutes

Total Time: 60 minutes

Serve: 3

Calories: 221 kcal

Ingredients:

- 1 Cup of dried cranberries
- ½ Bag of dark chocolate chips
- 1 Yellow cake mix
- 1 Tbsp. pumpkin pie spice
- 1 Can pumpkin

Cooking Instructions:

1. In a medium mixing bowl, merge together all the ingredients. Mix well pour the mixture into the Ninja Foodi pan.

2. Lay it on the basket. Put the pressure lid on and be sure the valve is in seal position. Select high pressure and set to cook for 50 minutes.

3. When the cooking cycle is up, do quick pressure release for 10 minutes. Open the lid and transfer the cake to a serving plate.

4. Serve and enjoy!!!

Apple Cobbler

Preparation Time: 10 minutes

Cook Time: 25 minutes

Total Time: 35 minutes

Serve: 2

Calories: 229 kcal

Ingredients:

- 2 Cups of apples, diced
- 2 Cups of milk
- 2 Cups of sugar
- 2 Cups of flour
- 2 Tbsp. of butter, melted
- Cinnamon to taste
- Vanilla to taste

Cooking Instructions:

1. In a medium mixing bowl, merge together all the ingredients except the apple. Mix well and pour the mixture into the Ninja Foodi pan.

2. Place apples on the mixture. Put the pressure lid on and be sure the valve is in seal position. Select high pressure and set to cook for 25 minutes.

3. When the cooking cycle is up, do quick pressure release for 10 minutes. Open the lid and transfer the cake to a serving plate.

4. Serve and enjoy!!!

Banana Cupcakes

Preparation Time: 10 minutes

Cook Time: 25 minutes

Total Time: 35 minutes

Serve: 2

Calories: 229 kcal

Ingredients:

- 3 Large bananas
- 1 Box of cake mix

Cooking Instructions:

1. Begin by mashing the bananas in a small mixing bowl and then put the cake mix. Give it a good mix.

2. Share the mixture into cupcake pan and arrange them on the Ninja Foodi basket. Put the pressure lid on and be sure the valve is in seal position.

3. Select high pressure and set to cook for 20 minutes. When the cooking cycle is up, do quick pressure release for 10 minutes.

4. Serve and enjoy!!!

Chocolate Lava Cake

Preparation Time: 10 minutes

Cook Time: 2 hours 30 minutes

Total Time: 2 hours 40 minutes

Serve: 2

Calories: 229 kcal

Ingredients:

Cake:

- 1 Box Betty Crocker Super Moist triple chocolate fudge cake mix
- 1¼ Cups of milk
- ½ Cup of vegetable oil
- 3 Eggs

Topping:

- 1 Box of instant chocolate pudding and pie filling mix
- 2 Cups of milk
- 1 Bag of (12 Oz.) milk chocolate chips

Cooking Instructions:

1. Begin by spraying the Ninja Foodi basket with cooking spray. Using a large mixing bowl, beat the cake Ingredients using electric mixer.

2. Pour the mixture into the Ninja Foodi. Merge together pudding mix and milk in a medium mixing bowl and pour into the Ninja Foodi over the cake mixture.

3. Do not mix. Top with chocolate chips. Put the pressure lid on and be sure the valve is in seal position.

4. Select high pressure and set to cook on slow cook low for 2 hours 30 minutes. When the cooking cycle is up, do quick pressure release for 10 minutes.

5. Serve and enjoy!!!

Lightning Source UK Ltd.
Milton Keynes UK
UKHW050742050321
379837UK00013B/1700

9 781952 504686